The Volume of Payments and the Informal Economy in the Netherlands 1965-1982

W.C. Boeschoten and Prof. dr. M.M.G. Fase

The Volume of Payments and the Informal Economy in the Netherlands 1965 - 1982

An attempt at quantification

Monetary Monographs No. 1

1984 De Nederlandsche Bank n.v.
Martinus Nijhoff Publishers, Dordrecht

ISBN-13:978-90-247-3095-7 e-ISBN-13:978-94-009-5059-7
DOI:10.1007/978-94-009-5059-7

Distributors
For the United States and Canada: Kluwer Academic Publishers,
190 Old Derby Street, Hingham, MA 02043, USA
For the UK and Ireland: Kluwer Academic Publishers, MTP Press Limited, Falcon House,
Queen Square, Lancaster LA1 1RN, England
For all other countries: Kluwer Academic Publishers Group, Distribution Center,
P.O. Box 322, 3300 AH Dordrecht, The Netherlands

Contents

Preface of the President

1 Introduction 9

2 The available estimation methods 11
- 2.1 Direct or non-monetary methods 11
- 2.2 Indirect or monetary methods 13

3 Closer analysis of the transactions method 16

4 The volume of payments 19
- 4.1 Cash payments 19
- 4.2 Transfers 23

5 Estimations of the informal economy 26
- 5.1 A first estimation of the informal economy 26
- 5.2 The estimations in greater detail 28
- 5.3 Some estimations based on alternative assumptions 30
- 5.4 Application of a variant of the transactions method 31

6 Comparison with findings in the literature 34

7 Summary and conclusions 36

Appendix I Estimation of cash payments with the lifetime method 42
Appendix II The giro transfer system 47
Appendix III Amplification of bank transfers 50
Appendix IV Comparison with transactions as estimated by Cramer 52
Appendix V Estimation of total transactions 55
Appendix VI Survey of estimates of the size of the underground and the informal economies for a number of countries 64

Bibliography 68

Authors Index 74

Subject Index 75

Preface of the President

The Netherlands Bank has always considered it one of its duties, also in view of its responsibilities with regard to policy-making, to give a major impetus to research activities within the Bank, and to provide its researchers with the freedom which is indispensable for conducting scientific research. Many of the resulting studies have meanwhile found their way to national and international scientific journals. However, in view of the inevitable limitations which a journal article imposes upon, for example, the justification and the presentation of the data used, an alternative was sought and found in the brochure or monograph. With this background in mind, we now have before us the first of a series of monetary monographs to be published by the Bank. It reflects the desire of the Governing Board to make research work done by staff members accessible to a wider public. The fact that the series is published under the auspices of the Bank does not, however, necessarily mean that the authors' findings reflect the opinions held by the Bank.

The present study, by Prof. Dr. M.M.G. Fase and W.C. Boeschoten of the Econometric Research and Special Studies Department, makes a contribution to more extensive quantitative insight into the informal economy in the Netherlands. It must be emphasized that this study attempts to measure a phenomenon which finds its basis in the aim to conceal the underlying activities. The utmost caution should therefore be exercised when making use of the material presented here.

It gives me great pleasure to be able to introduce this first issue of the series of monetary monographs of the Netherlands Bank. It deals with the volume of payments and the informal economy in the Netherlands, a fascinating subject; the underlying statistics on payments were compiled especially for this study and are entirely new. I would like to take this opportunity to express our gratitude to the managing boards of the ABN, Amro-bank, NMB, Rabobank and the PCGD, who acceded to our request for acces to their administrative data on payments on behalf of this study. Without their generous cooperation this research could not have been carried out.

W.F. Duisenberg

1. Introduction

This study provides an estimate of the size of the informal economy in the Netherlands in the period 1965-1982. In this study the informal economy has been defined statistically as that part of the non-registered national product which involves monetary transactions. Bartering activities and transactions outside the market are thus left completely out of consideration. The same is true of those market transactions which, despite their illegal or underground nature, are already included in the national product published by the Central Bureau of Statistics (CBS) because of its measuring methods. According to the CBS (1983a) these transactions account for 5 to 10% of national income. This means that the estimate of the informal economy will be smaller when the statistical registration is more comprehensive and a wider starting point is chosen than the market. The term underground economy as used in a fiscal context therefore means something else than the statistical term informal economy used in this study [1].

The phenomenon of the informal economy emanates partly from the usual measuring conventions; at the same time it is also an expression of economic behaviour motivated by economic incentives and conditions which aims to keep such economic dealing concealed. This study attempts to quantify the size of that informal economy partly on the basis of economic behaviour. Observable monetary transactions were the main starting point. This implies that the transactions considered are limited to those which are effected in the market, a limitation which, incidentally, ensues entirely from the way in which the problem is formulated.

The first and foremost aim of this study is the estimation of the informal economy through an application of Feige's (1979) transactions method to the Netherlands. In this method a major role is played by observed payments. The present study should therefore be seen as a more or less unprecedented – at least in the Netherlands – attempt at statistical measurement. This does not mean that the criticism of this method voiced in the literature [2] is rejected. On the contrary, the application of this approach to the Netherlands means that it is being tested against the facts. The present study confirms, particularly since it covers a long period, the problems cited in the literature as being inherent in Feige's approach. Nevertheless, we agree with Heertje and Cohen (1980), as well as with Van Tuinen, – and this is the second

---

1 For a detailed definition the reader is referred to Van Tuinen (1981), Blokland (1982) and Van Eck (1983). See also Van Tuinen (1980) with regard to Heertje and Cohen (1980).

2 Cf. for example Cramer (1980, 1981b), Van Tuinen (1981), Tanzi (1982) and Pen (1983).

aim of the study – that no stone must be left unturned to obtain greater quantitative insight into the size of the informal economy and the quality of the measuring methods. This means that the plausibility of the outcomes of this study can only be assessed fully against the background of other approaches, in particular for the Netherlands, the on-going work of Van Bijsterveld (1980) and to some extent also that of the CBS, which follow a more direct approach than this study.

This study covers the years 1965-1982. During this period the total burden of taxation and social insurance contributions doubled to more than 50% of net national income. This burden is generally regarded as the most important determinant for the size of the informal economy. This justifies the presumption that, insofar as there is an informal economy, its growth will have taken place mainly in the period considered. The year 1965 was chosen as the first observation year because it is virtually, if not entirely, impossible to obtain the necessary data for the period prior to that year.

2 The available estimation methods

It is in the nature of things that the black economy, and thus the informal economy, too, remain unobservable. Quantification is therefore more of an approximation made on the basis of sometimes far-reaching assumptions. The available estimation methods can be roughly divided into two categories. For systematical reasons these are referred to below as the direct and indirect methods. For the time being the latter are based mainly on monetary statistics. It must be noted that it is not always clear whether the various methods are aims at estimating the black or the informal economy. In the following survey the two terms are used interchangeably.

2.1 Direct or non-monetary methods

The most direct approach, applied, for example, by the Internal Revenue Service (1979) for the United States, Frank (1977) for Belgium and recently the CBS (1983b) for the Netherlands, is the fiscal or discrepancy method. This method compares the national income as presented in the National Accounts, which has been estimated on the basis of data on expenditure and output, with income as it is derived from fiscal data. This size of the black economy therefore equals the unexplained difference between the national incomes presented by these two sources. The CBS puts this difference for the income of households in the Netherlands in 1977 at 6½ % or over Fl. 12 billion. The CBS estimates that the volume of capital income was Fl. 5 billion or 30 % greater than the amount derivable from the tax data. A problem which arises here is that both statistical sources are inevitably subject to inaccuracies, and do not necessarily dovetail. In addition, this method only looks at that part of registered national income which is not declared to the tax authorities. Non-registered income is left out of consideration. As a consequence, the method estimates only the lower limit for the black economy.

The same objection can be made as regards estimates which are based on the outcomes of *tax auditing*. There, too, non-registered income is – at least partly – left out of account. Furthermore, tax auditing will, on average, not expose all black activities. Another problem is that, generally speaking, such investigations will be aimed mainly at fraud-sensitive sectors, a factor which detracts from the representativeness of the outcomes.

Closely in line with this method, *micro-economic approaches* attempt to gain insight into the size of the black economy by means of random samples and surveys. This system is used in the Netherlands by the CBS to obtain a more refined registration of national income. For example, the CBS recently held two experimental surveys on black expenditure among consumers [3]. In order to estimate the total size of the informal sector, the estimates for the separate components must be totalled. The compilation and aggregation of the relevant micro-economic data are accompanied by vast practical problems and considerable cost. Furthermore, the danger of underestimation looms large, and it is usually impossible to reconstruct data for the past with this method. It is consequently well-nigh impossible to estimate developments regarding the black economy over an extended period with this method. As a gauge for estimates obtained through other methods, however, the estimates obtained by means of this approach provide valuable information. In addition, the micro-economic data can afford insight into the quantitative importance of alleged determinants of tax evasion. Clotfelter (1983), for example, deduces from the results of a fiscal study made by the IRS in 1969 that a 10 % decline in the marginal tax rate leads to a 5 to 8 % decrease of tax evasion. Isachsen *et al.* (1982) have calculated from the results of random samples taken in Norway in 1980 that a 1 % increase in the probability of detection will lead to a 2 % decline in black activities.

A totally different approach is provided by the *sensitivity analysis* applied by Van Tuinen (1980, 1981) and Broesterhuizen (1983). This method admittedly does not result in concrete estimates, but it does make it possible to test the plausibility of the available estimates. Thus Van Tuinen reaches the surprising conclusion that in the Netherlands at least 55 % of the national product is achieved in fraud-sensitive sectors such as the public sector, public sector enterprises or sectors of industry whose contribution to the national product has been estimated with fraud-insensitive estimation methods. As a consequence, the estimated informal economy is, in this view, concentrated entirely in those sectors where the remaining 45 % are produced [4]. On the basis of his sensitivity analysis for 1979, Broesterhuizen considers it improbable that the distortion of the national product through fraud exceeds 5 %. He puts the distortion of the growth at no more than ½ percentage point per year. Similar estimates, where the presumed fraud-intensity in the various sectors is weighted with their shares in the national income, were recently made for other countries. The results show fairly great similarity [5]. Apart from the fact that sensivity analyses do not yield con-

[3] These showed, among other things, that about 12 % of car maintenance was in the form of black activities. For hairdressing the share was less than 10 %, while the black component of wages paid for house repairs and renovation came out at over 20 % Blokland (1982).

[4] Feige's (1980) estimate for the United States, which comes out at 27 % of GNP, would mean, for the Netherlands, that 60 % of production in the fraud-sensitive sectors of industry remains statistically unobserved. This seems an implausible outcome.

[5] Fisher (1982) puts the Australian informal economy at, at most, 5 % of GNP, the same percentage found by Broesterhuizen for the Netherlands. Rose (1983) and Frey and Weck (1983) estimated percentages of 4-7.2 and 2.7 for England and Switzerland respectively in 1975.

crete estimates, the main objection to this method is that the distinction between fraud-sensitive and fraud-insensitive sectors seems rather arbitrary. In addition, criminal activities such as those estimated by Blades (1983) at 2-3 % of GNP for the United States in 1975, are left out of consideration in this methodology.

Finally there is also the *causal method* used by Frey *et al.* (1981, 1982, 1983). These authors postulate a connection between the size of the black economy and a number of determinants such as the burden of taxation and social insurance contributions, the degree of regulation, tax morality, available time off and the rate of unemployment. It is on the basis of this assumed relationship that the authors determine the growth of the black economy. The difference in the size of the black economy in the various countries can be explained analogously. Frey's estimates are on the whole quite plausible. This is, incidentally, hardly surprising since they evolve entirely from factors which are assumed *ex ante* to determine developments regarding the black economy. This *ad hoc* basis is the weak point in this approach. Frey and Weck recently attempted to quantify the influence of the above factors on the size of the informal economy in seventeen OECD countries. For the years 1960-1978 they found a significant influence only for the burden of direct taxes, tax morality and the degree of regulation.

2.2. Indirect or monetary methods

Most published estimates of the black economy are obtained via the so-called indirect methods. Apart from a few exceptions [6], these are based on monetary statistics, supplemented with behavioural hypotheses about the money-using economy. Furthermore, it is assumed that the measuring of monetary data is not influenced by the presence of a black circuit. Monetary statistics are assumed to comprise both 'white' and 'black' components. The size of the black economy – expressed throughout as a percentage of GNP – follows from the degree in which the actual value of the monetary quantity considered deviates from its expected or normal value. The difference observed is imputed to the black or informal economy. This is a major simplification which precludes other explanations for this difference, such as institutional factors. In this connection it is of major importance to distinguish sharply between the black and the informal economy.

The most straightforward example of the monetary approach is Gutmann's (1977) *currency-ratio method*. This method relies on an – in principle – constant ratio of cash to

---

[6] One of these exceptions is the so-called *Italian method*, which is based on statistics on participation in the labour market. This method estimates the size of the black economy from the difference between the observed and the normative rate of participation in the labour market. The method, which also covers the black barter economy, has so far been applied mainly to Italy.

demand deposits. Furthermore, it assumes that informal transactions are always effected in cash, with the income velocity of cash equalling that of money (M_1) in the official economy. In this view, the rise in the ratio between cash and demand deposits observable in the United States since the early 1960s is implicitly and entirely attributed to the growth of the informal economy. For the United States, Gutmann comes up with an underground economy of nearly 10% of GNP for 1976.

The plausibility of the assumptions underlying Gutmann's method can be called in question for several reasons. In the first place, black transactions may in part be paid via transfers. In fact, this is the case for some 25-30% of black transactions effected in the United States, according to a study made in 1979 by the International Revenue Service. A similar percentage was found for Norway by Isachsen *et al.* (1982). Secondly, the income velocity of cash in the informal sector presumably deviates from the relevant income velocity in the official sector. In view of the far-reaching institutional changes undergone by the financial system during the past twenty years or so, the third and most important objection to this method is that it assumes a constant ratio of cash to demand deposits.

This very restrictive assumption is abandoned in the so-called *Tanzi-method*, which was inspired by a study made by Cagan (1958). This approach explains the ratio of cash to demand deposits (or a broader concept of liquidity) by means of a behavioural equation. This equation comprises not only variables such as interest rates and income, but also one or more variables – usually the burden of taxation and social insurance contributions – in order to be able to approximate the influence of tax evasion. The size of the black economy is subsequently derived from the extra demand for cash which must be attributed to tax evasion according to the estimated equation. As in the case of Gutmann's approach, a serious objection is that in Tanzi's view black transactions are paid exclusively in cash. Furthermore, the income velocity of the payment methods used in both sectors is assumed to be the same. The basically variable relationship between currency and total money supply is, however, an attractive aspect of Tanzi's approach. The results, on the other hand, are rather sensitive to the specification of the behavioural equation used. This becomes very clear in, for example, the application of a variant of this method to Canada by Mirus and Smith (1982).

The above objections to the monetary approach are partly counteracted by the *transactions method* developed by Feige (1979). This method is based on a normal and constant ratio between the total amount involved in transactions PT and the income Y involved in these transactions. In conformity with Fisher's equation of exchange – *i.e.* $MV = PT$ – the transactions amount PT is equated with the total of cash payments and transfers MV, with M the primary money stock, T the volume of transactions, P the price level and V the implicity defined velocity of circulation. In principle, MV also comprises black payments. Insofar as the observed ratio of total transactions MV to registered income Y exceeds the normal ratio, this is attributed to the informal economy.

The disadvantage of this method is that, as in the case of Gutmann's approach, a certain relationship, in this case PT/Y, must be considered constant. Another objection, which incidentally holds for all monetary methods, is that the estimates obtained relate solely to the non-registered economy. That part of the black economy included in the national product as a result of the measuring method is consequently left out of account. A great advantage of the method is that it does not exclude the possibility that black transactions are paid via transfers. In addition, this approach is not distorted as a result of shifts between cash payments and transfers brought about by, for example, institutional changes.

In summary, the estimation method proposed by Feige seems sufficiently attractive to warrant closer scrutiny and application. Owing to the absence of statistics on transfers, the determination of MV for a number of years poses greater problems for the Netherlands than, for example, for the United States and the United Kingdom. The following sections therefore deal extensively with the determination of MV. First, however, a closer look will be taken at Feige's transactions method, which forms the basis for the present study.

3 Closer analysis of the transactions method

The transactions method assumes a normal and constant ratio of total transactions PT to total national income Y. In view of the aims of this study, the transactions total PT is measured by total cash payments and transfers MV. The excess, in a given year, of the observed ratio MV/Y over the ratio considered normal is attributed to informal transactions [7].

The crux of the transactions method is the assumption of a normal, and – over time – constant ratio of total transactions PT to total income Y. This assumption is very common to macro-economic monetary theory. Yet, apart from changes in the size of the informal economy, there are at least two other reasons why the transactions income ratio need not be constant over time.

The first could be a progressing integration of the production process [8] or a relative expansion of the services sector. This causes the number of transactions per unit of output to decline and with it the ratio of PT to Y. A second reason for variability in time could be diverging movements in prices for newly produced end products and for all goods and services.

In table 1 an attempt is made to test these two arguments against actual developments. The steadily declining share of intermediary transactions indicates a progressing integration of the production process. As the second column shows, the share of services in GNP has increased markedly. Both these developments detract from the assumption of a constant ratio of total transactions to income.

As for the movements in price relationships, Table 1 shows that of the four price index numbers given, only that for existing plus (part of the) newly built dwellings has risen faster than the GNP deflator [9].

---

[7] If the observed income is written as Y^{o}, the unobserved income Y^{uo} is calculated as

$$Y^{uo} = Y - Y^{o} \quad \text{or} \quad Y^{uo} = \frac{MV}{\alpha_0} - Y^{o}$$

with α_0 the ratio MV/Y^{o} in the normative base year. In that year the size of the unobserved economy is considered negligible or known. Incidentally this means that, under these circumstances, the ratio MV/Y is just as large in the unobserved economy as in the observed economy.

[8] In their studies of the velocity of circulation of money, Holtrop (1928) and Zijlstra (1948) used the concept differentiation coefficient in this context.

[9] In view of the limited quantitative importance of sales in the market for dwellings – at Fl. 24 billion in the peak year of 1974 less than 2% of the eventually estimated transactions total PT – the above-mentioned integral price relationship will nevertheless have declined in the period considered.

Table 1
Degree of integration, share of services in GNP and price relationships, 1965-1982

	Share of inter-mediary in final trans-actions	Share of services in GNP	Price relationship			
			cost of living and GNP	domestic sales and GNP	dwellings and GNP	second-hand cars and GNP
1965	0.55	0.38	1.06	1.17	1.01	1.51
1966	0.55	0.38	1.06	1.16	0.99	1.49
1967	0.54	0.39	1.04	1.10	0.95	1.45
1968	0.54	0.39	1.05	1.07	1.01	1.44
1969	0.52	0.37	1.05	1.05	0.99	1.39
1970	0.52	0.39	1.03	1.05	1.03	1.36
1971	–	0.39	1.03	1.01	1.03	1.30
1972	0.49	0.39	1.00	0.95	1.04	1.22
1973	0.48	0.39	1.01	0.97	1.11	1.16
1974	0.47	0.40	1.00	1.07	1.06	1.08
1975	0.48	0.41	1.00	1.00	1.00	1.00
1976	0.48	0.41	1.00	0.99	1.35	0.94
1977	0.45 [a]	0.45 [a]	1.00	0.97	1.68	0.91
1978	0.45	0.46	0.99	0.90	1.87	0.88
1979	0.42	0.46	0.99	0.93	1.78	0.87
1980	0.42	0.46	1.00	0.99	1.60	0.84
1981	–	0.46	1.01	1.07	1.35	0.82
1982	–	0.47	1.01	1.07	1.14	0.79

[a] Start of a new series owing to revision of the National Accounts.

Explanatory note
The figures have been calculated from data derived from the National Accounts and the Statistische Zakboekjes (Statistical Digests) of the CBS. The last column is also based partly on data from the Netherlands Association RAI.

The developments described in Table 1 therefore do not support the assumption of a constant ratio of total transactions to income. For this reason alone Feige's transactions method may not be applied to the Netherlands without amendment. Apart from this consideration, the ratio of total transactions, measured by MV, to income is also partially influenced by a varying share of non-current transactions in total monetary transactions. This gives rise to the possibility that a shift in the composition of net financial assets brought about by, for example, fluctuations in interest rate differentials, is seen as an expansion of the informal economy. This statistical measuring problem forms a major objection to application of the transactions method [10]. This

[10] Cramer (1980, 1981b) has pointed out that this is one of the reasons for Feige's exceptionally high estimate of the hidden economy in the United States. For Frey and Weck (1983) the impossibility to separate purely financial transactions is a reason not to apply the transactions method to Switzerland.

distortion could, however, be compensated for by excluding non-current transactions from the observed monetary transactions MV. To that end a distinction must be made between current and non-current transactions. Such a distinction is never unequivocal, because virtually every transaction is income generating [11].

In this article transactions are considered non-current if no income is generated or if the income generated is negligible with respect to the size of the transaction concerned [12]. Non-current transactions comprise three large groups of transactions. In the first place the purely *financial transactions*, of which transfers between accounts of one and the same account holder, the exchange of demand deposits for cash and vice versa, and transfers ensuing from banks' money market operations are notable examples [13].

Transactions which give rise to two or more transfers also belong to this category. They include gifts, inheritances, real estate transactions and other transactions made through the intermediation of a notary public and taking place via one of his accounts. Secondly, there are *capital transactions*, such as real estate dealings, the trade in second-hand cars, stock exchange transactions and redemptions. The third category is made up of *income transfers*, such as tax payments and income transfers on account of social security and pensions; these sometimes involve more than one transfer.

The next section provides an estimate of domestic transfers and cash payments. Part of the above financial transactions, viz. money market transactions, cash withdrawals from own accounts and double counting have been eliminated as far as possible. Section 5 will subsequently deal with the elimination of the remaining part of the other non-current transactions mentioned above. In addition, the transactions method is applied for several variants of the estimations, so as to yield an estimation of the informal economy in the Netherlands.

---

11 True exceptions are, for example, the exchange of the currency for another, and transfers between different accounts of one and the same account holder.

12 In the wake of Keynes, Zijlstra (1948) uses the terms 'industrial circulation' and 'financial circulation' in this connection.

13 Exchange of money for money, changing hands in the process, must be regarded as a current transaction. This goes notably for withdrawals from and deposits into accounts held by someone else.

4 The volume of payments

Payments are effected in cash or via transfers, which include guaranteed cheque payments. Total payments therefore equal the sum of cash payments and transfers. For the Netherlands the statistics on total monetary payments are incomplete. Fragmentary statistical information is available. To approximate the volume of cash payments in the Netherlands, Cramer (1978, 1981a) and Uyttewaal (1981) have made estimates for a number of years. As for the volume of transfers, only the volume of transfers at the Netherlands Bank has been published for the whole observation period from 1965 to 1982. Transfers recorded by the giro services were published regularly until 1980 [14], while those of the Banks' Clearing Institution were shown in the relevant annual reports, be it only as number of transactions. On the basis of this fragmentary statistical information, Cramer attempted earlier to estimate transfers for the years 1974-1978.

This section presents estimates of cash payments and transfers in a first attempt to determine the volume of total transactions. For this use could be made of data supplied by a number of individual banks. These form the basis for the following estimation.

4.1 Cash payments

To estimate cash payments, both the 'cash loop' method and the 'lifetime' method were used. The cash loop method developed by I. Fischer (1909), was applied to the Netherlands earlier by Cramer. The basic principles of the lifetime method were developed by Laurent (1970) for application in the US. In the Netherlands this method was applied earlier by Uyttewaal.

The basic starting-point for the cash loop method is the fact that notes and coin are brought into and taken out of circulation via the counters of banks and post and giro offices. The money circulation is, as it were, the loop between withdrawal and deposit. The length of this loop equals the number of net payments between withdrawal and deposit. Cash payments are the product of the length of the cash loop and the volume of cash withdrawals. The latter have been derived from the records of banks and giro institutions. Table 2 shows cash withdrawals for the years 1965-1982.

---

[14] In: Statistisch Jaarboek van PCGD/RPS (up to and including 1980); Maandstatistiek voor het Financiewezen (until October 1978) and Jaarboek van Amsterdam (up to and including 1978).

Table 2
Cash withdrawals at money-creating institutions and savings banks, 1965-1982 (billions of guilders) [1]

	From demand deposits at			From savings deposits	From time deposits	Total
	giro institutions, major banks and savings banks [2]	other banks	total			
1965	18.4	3.1	21.5	8.3	0.2	30.0
1966	20.1	3.2	23.3	9.4	0.2	32.9
1967	23.0	3.3	26.3	10.5	0.3	37.1
1968	27.5	3.8	31.2	11.4	0.4	43.0
1969	34.2	4.6	38.8	12.4	0.4	51.6
1970	41.2	4.3	45.6	14.2	0.5	60.4
1971	49.2	4.9	54.1	16.1	0.4	70.6
1972	56.8	6.2	63.0	17.4	0.4	80.7
1973	64.2	6.5	70.7	18.5	0.7	89.9
1974	74.6	6.4	81.0	15.3	1.2	97.5
1975	85.4	8.0	93.3	13.6	1.2	108.1
1976	95.5	7.8	103.3	13.7	1.5	118.5
1977	105.9	8.7	114.5	13.5	1.7	129.8
1978	111.9	8.7	120.6	14.3	1.8	136.6
1979	121.5	9.9	131.4	15.3	2.0	148.7
1980	130.4	10.5	140.9	17.0	2.2	160.2
1981	137.8	10.0	147.8	15.2	2.5	165.5
1982	144.3	10.3	154.6	16.0	2.7	173.3

[1] Including guaranteed cheques and Euro-cheques which have been cashed. As of 1971 cash withdrawals have been derived directly from the data provided. For earlier years these were mainly estimated from demand deposits, with the aid of equations estimated for the years 1971-1982 for the withdrawal frequency.

[2] Including cash withdrawals from checking accounts and savings accounts at savings banks. Strictly speaking these are monetarily neutral. Cramer's (1981a) estimation therefore comprises only withdrawals from savings accounts at banks, which are estimated to make up about 60 % of total withdrawals from savings banks. It is, however, not assumable that savings taken up at banks are spent differently from savings taken up elsewhere. In pinciple the inclusion of cash withdrawals at savings banks leads to a shorter cash loop.

According to this estimate, over Fl. 140 billion worth of cash was taken up in 1980 from demand deposits at giro institutions, banks and savings banks. With deposits averaging Fl. 45.6 billion at these institutions, this means a rate of turnover of 3.1.

The total amount involved in cash withdrawals from demand deposits, savings accounts and time deposits came to over Fl. 160 billion in 1980. With the assumption of a cash loop of 2, cash payments would thus total Fl. 320 billion. This corresponds to more than 1½ times the measured personal consumption in that year. This seems reasonable because, apart from a considerable share of this consumption, business transactions are also partly paid in cash. Nevertheless there is little certainty about the length of the cash loop. In his time Fisher put it at 1.5. Cramer uses a value of 2. In view of the outcome of a survey conducted for the Netherlands Bank about the way in which people obtain cash, a cash loop of 2 seems rather on the ample side. Nevertheless, as a start and by way of a working hypothesis, a cash loop of 2 was assumed. Section 5 will deal with this assumption in greater detail, when estimating the size of the informal economy. Incidentally, the above cash withdrawals amounting to Fl. 160 billion in 1980, with an assumed cash loop of 2 and an amount of currency in circulation of Fl. 21.0 billion, imply a velocity of circulation for currency of over 15.

Contrary to the cash loop method, Laurent's lifetime method uses as its basis means of payment, especially banknotes. It assumes that a fixed number, say G, payments can be made with each banknote before it is soiled and taken out of circulation. With an average lifetime of L years, on average G/L payments are made per year with each banknote. Thus the intensity with which a denomination is used is assumed to be inversely proportional to its lifetime. Since the latter declines as the denomination decreases, this means that small denominations are, on average, used more intensively than large denominations. Likewise, the decrease of the average lifetime observed for four out of five denominations is, in this view, solely the result of an increase in the intensity with wich they are used (see Appendix I). Multiplication of the average number of payments per year G/L with the relevant circulation value yields the total amount of payments made with the denomination concerned. Summation for the various denominations yields the payments made with banknotes in a certain year. Thus a series expressed in terms of G has been drawn up for total cash payments; the quantitatively fairly unimportant circulation of coin is left out of consideration. By equating the value found for 1980 with cash payments of Fl. 320 billion calculated for that year with the aid of the cash loop method, a series of amounts was subsequently derived from this index series [15]. These amounts increase from over Fl. 100 billion to Fl. 350 billion over the period considered.

Chart 1 presents cash payments as calculated with the two different estimation methods and expressed in terms of GNP. It shows that until 1971 developments in this relationship differ widely for the two methods. However, as from 1971 there is a large measure of correspondence. Developments regarding cash payments estimated with the lifetime method seem the most plausible until 1971, because they reflect the declining significance of cash payments during this period. That is why the rest of this study is based on the cash payments estimations as calculated with Laurent's lifetime method.

---

[15] The method used, the calculation of the lifetime and the results are explained in greater detail in Appendix I.

Chart 1
Estimates of cash payments in relationship to GNP (cash loop = 2), 1965-1982

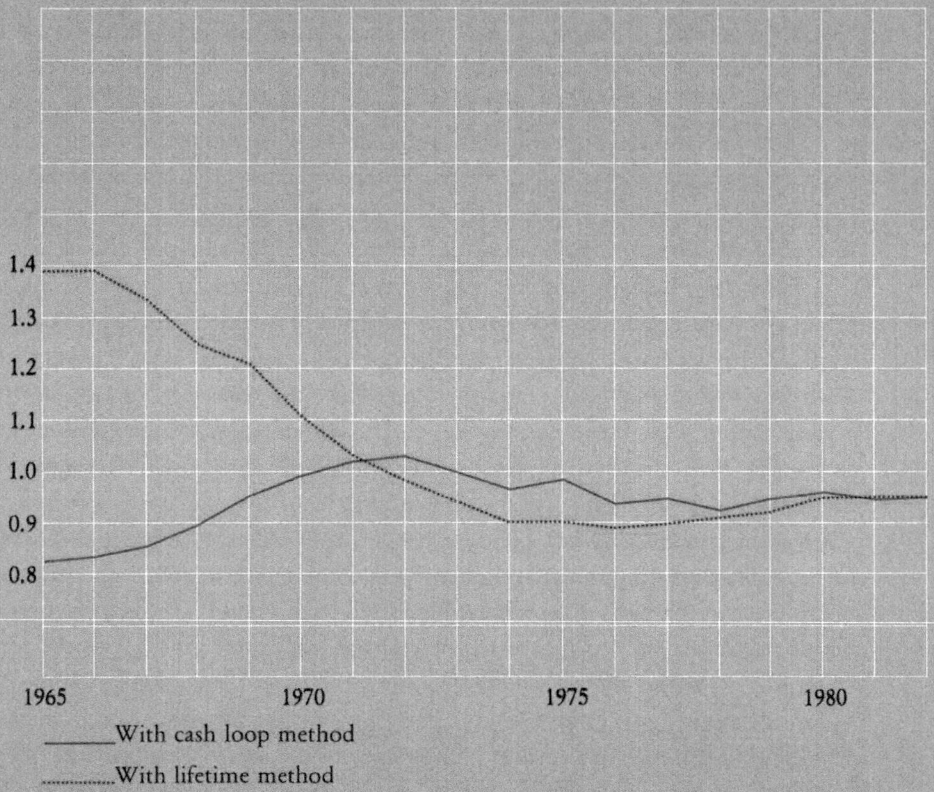

It may be pointed out that the results obtained with the lifetime method do not necessarily have to be inconsistent with the estimates derived from cash withdrawals with the aid of the cash loop method. If a cash loop is assumed which, instead of having a constant value of 2, declines in the first period and subsequently rises slightly in the second, developments regarding cash payments will be the same as those found with the lifetime method.

4.2 Transfers

The relevant transfers take place mainly within and between two separate circuits: viz. that of the banks and that of the postal giro institution. The giro system of the Netherlands Bank forms the ultimate link between these two circuits.

The banks' circuit is made up of the banks and other institutions which provide giro facilities apart from the postal giro services. The most important of these, in quantitative terms, participate in the Banks' Clearing Institution set up in 1967 to facilitate the banks' transfers.

The circuit of the postal giro services is made up of all holders of postal giro accounts, including the public authorities, the Netherlands Bank, the other banks and the Banks' Clearing Institution.

Transfers between the two circuits take place partly via the Banks' Clearing Institution and partly directly via the banks' postal giro accounts and their accounts at the Netherlands Bank. In addition, transfers take place within the two circuits, and, within the Bank's giro system, between the banks, the postal giro services, the central government and others holding accounts at the Netherlands Bank (see Appendix II for a more detailed description).

As a large number of transfers take place via the Netherlands Bank, it is logical to derive their volume from the Bank's data. However, these transfers relate partly to net payments. Furthermore, they consist to a major and non-constant extent of financial transactions and payments into intermediary accounts which give rise to double counting. That is the reason why the Netherlands Bank's giro circuit is not a very practical basis. A second possible starting point is the total of transfers at giro institutions and the Banks' Clearing Institution. These are, however, incomplete as not all in- and intra bank payments take place via these institutions [16]. That is why in this paper transfers are measured directly, on the basis of debits at the banking system and giro services. To calculate debits at giro institutions use was made of published figures or of

[16] In conformity with Cramer's (1978) approach, these might be estimated on the basis of totals recorded at the Banks' Clearing Institution. In view of the large volume of unknown payments for 1977 – Cramer estimates them at nearly two-thirds of the Institution's transactions – and the far-reaching assumptions which must be made, such an approach seems less suitable for the long sample period – especially because the Institution only started to operate during that period.

data made available for this study. Debits at banks were derived from data on debits supplied for this study by a number of large banks at the request of the Bank. Total domestic debits at banks were obtained by raising their totals in accordance with their share in the total amount of demand deposits held at the banks, which was nearly 85 % in 1980. Taking into consideration double counting, this total plus the transfers at giro services and savings banks yield an estimate of total domestic transfers in the Netherlands [17], which is given in Table 3. It needs no mention that the estimation of the transfers of the smaller banks, implicit in the method of estimating total domestic debits,introduces an extra element of uncertainty (for the problems regarding this scaling see Appendix III).

Table 3
Estimation of debits in the Netherlands, 1965-1982
(billions of guilders)

	Debits at giro institutions and banks	Central government transfers	Payments to foreign countries	Total debits
1965	350.5	17.8	29.2	397.5
1966	384.6	19.8	31.5	435.9
1967	410.4	22.5	33.4	466.3
1968	459.8	25.5	37.6	522.9
1969	544.1	28.6	43.5	616.2
1970	611.6	31.6	54.5	697.7
1971	719.0	36.5	62.4	817.9
1972	795.9	42.1	63.1	901.1
1973	892.5	47.2	78.3	1,018.0
1974	1,006.7	55.8	105.9	1,168.4
1975	1,126.8	68.5	108.1	1,303.4
1976	1,242.2	80.7	124.0	1,446.9
1977	1,357.4	89.2	135.3	1,581.9
1978	1,494.4	103.6	141.1	1,739.1
1979	1,647.0	112.0	165.1	1,924.1
1980	1,809.8	120.2	196.4	2,126.4
1981	1,923.6	130.3	214.6	2,268.5
1982	2,018.1	143.8	222.5	2,384.4

Explanatory note
Cashed guaranteed cheques and Euro-cheques have not been included in total debits, but are regarded as part of cash payments. The amount involved is, incidentally, very small and does not exceed 0.5 % of total transfers.

---

[17] Transfers from checking accounts at savings banks have also been taken into account here.

The figures given in the first column of Table 3, which shows total debits minus the amounts of cashed guaranteed cheques and Euro-cheques derived from the Banks' Clearing Institution, do not yet include the central government's transfers [18]. The relevant total has been equated with central government expenditure on a cash basis, minus the central government's payments to foreign countries.

The still missing transfers to foreign countries have been approximated by totalling all imports of goods and services, and factor income and income transfers to foreign countries on a cash basis. Insofar as these payments are made in cash and in guilders, this approach involves double counting, as they were already included in the estimated cash payments. At an average of around Fl. 3 billion in 1980-1982, the volume of cash payments in guilders to foreign countries seems, however, slight for the time being. The last column of Table 3 shows the resulting transfers which incidentally are much higher for the relevant years than Cramer's estimates (see also Appendix IV).

Despite attempts to eliminate financial transactions as much as possible from the debits, the figures given in Table 3 form only a tentative approximation of actual non-financial debits. Thus it proved impossible to eliminate transfers between two accounts of one and the same account holder. Battelle's (1976) study shows that in the Netherlands many families hold more than one account. The same phenomenon is discernable in the business sector. The transfers concerned presumably involve considerable amounts of money. The estimated figures given in Table 3 are therefore exagerated on that account. In other respects they have, however, been underestimated. Thus, for example, transfers between account holders of the Netherlands Bank other than banks, postal giro service and central government are not included in the figures. The same is true of cash withdrawals from non-own accounts as these cannot always be distinguished from cash withdrawals from own accounts, which are not regarded as cash payments in this study. The estimation of the informal economy in section 5 explores a number of the above uncertainties in greater detail.

---

[18] Treasury transfers to bank accounts usually take place direct via the accounts of the relevant banks at the Netherlands Bank. An exception to this rule are payments which take place via bank accounts of 'intermediaries' such as municipalities. In that case, central government expenditure is as yet included in the banks' debits. Central government payments to postal giro accounts have been eliminated from the giro institutions' transfers as much as possible for the sake of uniformity.

5 Estimations of the informal economy

This section presents an estimate of the informal economy in the Netherlands obtained with the transactions method. As the outcome of this technique is largely determined by the assumptions made, an attempt is also made to ascertain to what extent the estimates change when some of the assumptions are modified. When drawing conclusions from the figures, it is of great importance to keep in mind the inextricability of the estimates and their underlying hypotheses.

5.1 A first estimation of the informal economy

The cash payments and transfers estimated in the preceding section yield the totals, MV, required for the application of the transactions method. On the basis of a normal ratio of MV to national income, a first estimation can be made of the informal economy as the difference between the actual and the normal ratio. The lowest ratio was taken as the normal one. This prevents one or more years from showing a negative informal economy. Table 4 gives the relevant estimate as a percentage of GNP, with 1976 as the base year. This choice means that it is assumed that there was no informal economy in 1976. Because this hypothesis must be regarded as too far-reaching, the size of the informal economy has been systematically underestimated pro tanto for all other years. As a consequence, Table 4 also presents an alternative estimation on the assumption that the size of the informal economy had been 5 % of GNP in 1976. This value has been derived from a very rough and tentative estimation of the black money circuit at end-1975 [19].

The developments found with regard to the informal economy, notably the initial relative decline until the second half of the 1970s, are a most surprising and not very plausible outcome. A decline as a percentage of GNP does not, however, necessarily mean a decrease in absolute terms. This becomes clear when we look at the results given in the third column, which show, on the basis of the alternative estimation in the second column, the size of the informal economy in billions of guilders.

---

[19] It derives from a comparison of the circulation of 1000-guilder notes in the Netherlands and of 1000 and 500-Deutsche Mark notes in the Federal Republic of Germany in 1975. If it is assumed that the large denominations in Germany were not used for informal transactions in 1975, and that the relative circulation of these denominations does not deviate from that in the Netherlands in the absence of an informal economy, the result is an informal economy of over 4 % at end-1975. It needs no contention that the line of thought pursued is very simple and normative. This is reflected by the choice of 5 %. The line of thought followed here was applied before for internal use by Fase (1979).

Table 4
First estimation of the size of the informal economy, 1965-1982

	Base variant % of GNP	Alternative estimation % of GNP	Ditto, in bill. of guild.	Percentage growth of GNP	Rate of inflation
1965	4.3	9.5	6.9	11.5	5.9
1966	5.2	10.4	8.2	8.6	6.1
1967	2.0	7.1	6.1	10.0	4.2
1968	2.0	7.1	6.8	10.5	4.2
1969	4.8	10.0	10.8	13.4	6.3
1970	3.9	9.1	11.0	12.3	5.5
1971	6.2	11.5	15.7	13.0	8.5
1972	2.8	8.0	12.3	13.4	9.3
1973	0.6	5.6	10.0	14.9	8.4
1974	1.2	6.2	12.5	13.2	9.3
1975	3.3	8.4	18.6	9.0	11.2
1976	0	5	12.6	15.0	8.8
1977	0.4	5.4	14.9	8.9	6.4
1978	2.3	7.5	22.1	7.7	5.2
1979	6.1	11.4	36.0	6.4	4.1
1980	10.1	15.6	52.2	6.4	5.3
1981	11.8	17.4	61.1	4.8	5.6
1982	12.7	18.3	67.1	4.2	5.9

Apart from several exceptions, it turns out that the size of the informal economy, measured in guilders, increases steadily to over Fl. 67 billion in 1982. The question arises whether this is possible. Closer analysis of this estimate by variation in the assumptions made is therefore called for.

As far as the expansion of the informal sector as a percentage of GNP is concerned, it can by no means be assumed that the informal economy always grows faster than the official economy. Especially in periods of a high nominal growth, partly in conjunction with a high rate of inflation, it seems plausible that the growth of the informal economy lags behind the expansion of the official economy [20]. The high rates of growth and inflation in the period 1965-1976 (last two columns in table 4) could be one of the reasons for the relative decline of the informal economy.

[20] This line of thought corresponds with the views of, among others, Molevski (1982) that it is notably in periods of recession that attempts are made to counteract a fall in income by means of black activities. O'Higgins (1982), on the other hand, is of the opinion that the black economy will undergo a relative expansion especially during boom-periods. O'Higgins' (1983) findings suggest, however, on the basis of estimates available on the informal economy in the United Kingdom, the Federal Republic of Germany, Canada and the United States, that there is no clear link between the expansion of the underground economy and that of the official economy.

Finally, it must be noted that a remarkable increase in underground activities in a number of so-called fraud-sensitive sectors will not necessarily lead to an expansion of the informal economy. The latter also depends on the relative significance of growth in the other sectors.

Nevertheless, there is a reasonable chance that the developments in the informal economy found for the years 1965-1982 are the result of the fact that the normal MV/Y ratio is incorrectly assumed to be constant. This ratio has, as already noted, presumably declined as a result of structural changes in the economy. This assumption, and several others, will be subjected to closer analysis in the following section.

5.2 The estimations in greater detail

Apart from changes in the velocity of circulation as a result of changes in the structure of the economy, the 'normal' relationship may have been influenced by diverging developments in different categories of transactions. Notable examples are non-current transactions which, with the exception of financial non-current transactions, are still included in the estimated totals. It seems advisable that the figures be adjusted accordingly. Incidentally, it may be wondered why they were not adjusted immediately. The main reason for separate consideration is that the estimation of such adjustments requires a number of – often far-reaching – additional assumptions. It is therefore more practical to consider them separately.

A first category of non-current transactions eligible for elimination is that of *income transfers.* These comprise contributions to social insurance funds, pension funds and assurance companies, benefits, tax payments and income and capital transfers. The 'output' of the public authorities has been substracted from this total. The resulting total income transfers have increased ninefold in the observation period, from Fl. 29 billion to Fl. 273 billion (see Appendix V).

A category of non-current transactions, also included in the total, which are even more difficult to estimate are the transfers from giro accounts to savings accounts, time deposits etc. Transfers to savings accounts have been estimated from the known total of deposits. Conversions into near money (excluding liquid savings) have been estimated from the totals of the various forms assuming average terms of 0.20-0.25 year. For practical reasons it has been assumed that credits to savings accounts and time deposits find their counterpart in debits to giro accounts. This means that it has been assumed that there are no direct transfers between savings accounts and time deposits. This is not a realistic assumption. It results in a rather erratic series which increases in the period considered from Fl. 30 billion to Fl. 337 billion.

Finally there is also the less sharply distinguishable category of *capital transactions.* This is a very heterogeneous group made up of among other things, real estate purchases, the trade in second-hand cars, inheritances, gifts and repayments on mortgages and consumer credit. The transaction totals involved have been roughly estimated. Nevertheless the estimation gives an impression of their quantitative significance. During the observation period the relevant totals increased tenfold, from Fl. 18 billion to Fl. 187 billion (see Appendix V).

The estimates of the informal economy which are obtained with the transactions method, after cumulative elimination of the above non-current transactions, are given in Table 5. In these estimates it has been assumed throughout that the minimum size of the informal economy is 0%, which is a fairly far-reaching assumption.

The successive eliminations highlight the decline found earlier for the informal economy which took place in the years prior to 1975. After 1975 the relative size of the informal economy sometimes turns out to be smaller. The results for the second period are relatively robust, at least compared with the years before 1976. The most extreme alternative estimates for, for example 1982, still differ by more than Fl. 12 billion.

Table 5
Size of the informal economy estimated with adjusted figures, 1965-1982 (% of GNP)

	Base variant	Excluding income transfers	Ditto, also excluding transfers to savings accounts etc.	Ditto, also excluding capital transactions
1965	4.3	8.7	15.9	21.1
1966	5.2	9.2	17.0	22.8
1967	2.0	5.4	12.2	16.9
1968	2.0	5.1	9.3	11.9
1969	4.8	8.1	13.1	16.5
1970	3.9	6.8	11.5	14.8
1971	6.2	8.9	15.2	18.9
1972	2.8	4.8	11.4	13.5
1973	0.6	1.8	6.5	8.8
1974	1.2	2.4	3.6	7.1
1975	3.3	3.7	5.3	7.7
1976	0	0	0.7	1.4
1977	0.4	0.3	0	0
1978	2.3	1.8	2.0	1.1
1979	6.1	5.8	6.2	7.5
1980	10.1	9.7	10.2	12.1
1981	11.8	11.2	10.4	11.2
1982	12.7	11.9	10.0	9.3

5.3 Some estimations based on alternative assumptions

In order to obtain a more detailed analysis of the sensitivity of the preceding estimates, four more estimations are given which are based on slightly different assumptions.

In the first place, Table 6 (second column) shows the development of the informal economy based on an estimation of transfers which results from a different way of amplifying the banks' transfers. Instead of basing the estimation on the velocity of circulation of demand deposits of one bank, which is supposed to be representative of the other banks, it was based on the average velocity of circulation of the demand deposits of the observed four major banks combined (see Appendix III for details). The estimated size of the informal economy then comes out nearly 2 percentage points lower for 1982, amounting to a slightly higher level, expressed as a percentage of GNP, than that found for the first year 1965. A more important aspect is, however, that in this case developments regarding the informal economy change markedly over the years considered.

Secondly, the development of the informal economy has been calculated on the basis of an estimation of cash payments with a cash loop of 1½ instead of the 2 assumed thusfar. Contrary to the first years since 1976, the size of the informal economy consequently turns out to be only slightly higher, if at all [21].

Thirdly, an attempt was made to investigate how sensitive the outcomes are to the assumption made on page 20 with regard to the estimate of cash payments on the lifetime of the various denominations. With a constant lifetime the size of the informal economy comes out 1 percentage point lower in 1982 (fourth column of Table 6). An estimation where in addition all denominations are given the same lifetime yields virtually the same results. It must be noted that in that case cash payments are proportional to the currency in circulation.

Finally, the development of the informal sector was calculated on the assumption that transactions in this sector are always made in cash. The last column of Table 6 shows that this would result in a smaller informal economy as of 1976. In 1982 it would have been 6½% of GNP or Fl. 24 billion. Given the earlier estimation, this means that roughly half the informal transactions in 1982 were effected in cash. It must be noted that this is a somewhat speculative interpretation.

---

[21] The outcome is contrary to the suggestion put forward by Feige, among others, that the larger the cash loop (velocity of circulation) assumed the higher the estimations found. The expansion of cash payments rising with a factor 3.4 was less sharp in the period observed than that of transfers, which increased nearly sixfold. A greater cash loop only provides the relatively less strongly increased cash payments with a greater weight in total transactions MV, with as a result a less strongly growing relationship MV/Y and thus a smaller estimated growth for the informal economy.

5.4 Application of a variant of the transactions method

The estimates of the informal economy derived from developments in the ratio of total payments to national product are underestimated insofar as the amount of current or real transactions ΣT_r per unit of GNP undergoes a structural decline, as the parallelism between total production and the total volume of current transactions is broken. That is the reason why developments in the underground economy have

Table 6
Alternative estimates of the informal economy, 1965-1982
(% of GNP)

	Base variant	With alternative amplification	With cash loop of 1½	With constant lifetime per denomination	Based on cash payments only
1965	4.3	9.3	2.5	7.8	54.9
1966	5.2	9.6	3.4	8.3	55.1
1967	2.0	5.9	0.4	4.7	48.9
1968	2.0	5.3	0.7	4.2	39.7
1969	4.8	7.2	3.7	6.6	35.9
1970	3.9	5.9	3.2	5.2	23.9
1971	6.2	7.1	5.8	7.2	16.6
1972	2.8	3.9	2.5	3.6	10.6
1973	0.6	1.4	0.4	1.1	5.2
1974	1.2	1.3	1.2	1.5	0.5
1975	3.3	3.5	3.4	3.4	1.2
1976	0	0	0	0	0
1977	0.4	0.1	0.4	0.2	0.3
1978	2.3	1.4	2.4	2.0	1.6
1979	6.1	5.5	6.2	5.6	3.3
1980	10.1	8.7	10.2	9.3	6.3
1981	11.8	10.4	12.0	10.8	6.4
1982	12.7	10.9	12.9	11.5	6.5

been estimated on the basis of the ratio $MV/\Sigma T_r$, instead of the ratio MV/Y, with total real transactions ΣT_r approximated on the basis of National Accounts figures [22]. The results are given in Table 7, with the different variants corresponding *mutatis mutandis* with those shown in Tables 5 and 6.

[22] Real transactions ΣT_r, which have been approximated from the end where sales and deliveries are made and money is received in return, include total industrial sales, the turnover of the wholesale and retail trade, wages and salaries, from investment income and entrepreneurial activities and the (approximated) 'output' of the public authorities. For a more detailed description see Appendix V.

A remarkable fact is that according to the base variant, the informal economy has increased steadily over the whole period observed. This result confirms the suspicion that the trough-like movements found when the orthodox transaction method are applied, are connected, at least partly, with structural changes in the Netherlands economy. According to the estimate obtained, the informal economy is supposed to have expanded to 22% of GNP, or Fl. 80 billion in the period 1965-1982. This is highly improbable, and only highlights the need for additional quantitative information for a better assessment of this result.

Table 7
Estimates of the informal economy on the basis of total volume of payments and current transactions
(% of GNP)

	Base-variant	Excluding income transfers	Excluding transfers	Excluding capital-transactions	With alternative amplification
1965	0	0	1.6	5.6	0
1966	1.7	1.3	3.5	8.0	1.0
1967	1.1	0.2	1.6	5.3	0.0
1968	2.2	1.0	0.0	2.0	0.6
1969	7.4	6.2	5.9	8.5	4.8
1970	6.2	4.7	4.2	6.8	3.3
1971	10.8	9.0	9.9	12.8	6.6
1972	11.4	9.0	10.4	11.9	7.4
1973	9.9	6.8	6.4	8.1	5.7
1974	8.3	5.2	1.4	4.3	3.4
1975	11.2	7.1	3.6	5.4	6.3
1976	8.7	4.2	0	0.2	3.6
1977	10.4	5.8	0.5	0	5.0
1978	13.5	8.4	3.4	2.0	7.3
1979	15.5	10.5	5.6	6.4	9.5
1980	17.5	12.3	7.5	8.8	10.7
1981	19.8	14.5	8.3	8.5	13.0
1982	22.0	16.2	8.9	7.6	14.5

As a result of the successive eliminations of non-current transactions from cash payments, the estimated size of the informal economy in 1982 turns out to be over 14 percentage points lower than the base variant, amounting to around 7½% of GNP. This means a size of nearly Fl. 28 billion for 1982, instead of the earlier estimate of Fl. 80 billion. Incidentally, the trough-like movements and the attending problem of which year to take as base year manifest themselves in their full extent in this variant.

Analogous with the second column of Table 6, the last column of Table 7 finally shows how sensitive the results are in this connection to the manner of amplification of the transfers included in MV.

6 Comparison with findings in the literature

Recent years have seen a variety of publications containing estimates of the size of the informal and the black economy. The measuring methods used in these estimates are as numerous as the definitions of the black economy. Additionally, the measuring point relates to different years. Nevertheless, Table 8 presents a survey of the outcomes for 17 OECD countries. These estimates have been obtained by applying one or more of the measuring methods described in section 2.

The transactions method used in this study has so far been applied by only three authors, for Canada, the Federal Republic of Germany, the United Kingdom and the United States. The resulting estimates, obtained with the transactions method, of the informal economy are high for all these countries, varying from around 15 % for

Table 8
Estimates of the size of the informal or the black economy in the literature
(% of GNP)

	Frey/Weck for 1978	Other authors	Year considered
Austria	8.9	3.8	1976
Belgium	12.1	11.0 - 20.8	1970; 1980
Canada	7.8	5.0 - 23.6	1976; 1980
Denmark	11.8	6.0	1974/1975
Fed. Rep. of Germany	8.6	3.7 - 27.0	1968; 1974; 1978; 1980
Finland	7.6	–	
France	9.4	6.7 - 23.2	1965; 1979
Ireland	7.2	8	1980
Italy	11.4	14 - 33	1977; 1978; 1979
Japan	4.1	–	
Netherlands	9.6	4 - 7	1977 t/m 1979; 1981
Norway	9.2	2.3 - 9.2	1978 t/m 1980; 1982; 1983
Spain	6.5	23	1978
Sweden	13.2	0.5 - 13.2	1970; 1976; 1978 t/m 1980
Switzerland	4.3	2.7 - 15.1	1975; 1978; 1980
United Kingdom	8.0	2 - 15	1970; 1977 t/m 1980
United States	8.3	1.4 - 28	1976 t/m 1982

Source: see Appendix VI.
Explanatory note:
It must be remembered that according to the definitions used in this article the informal and black economies are not synonymous.

Canada in 1980 and the United Kingdom in 1979, to 27 % for the Federal Republic of Germany in 1980 and the United States in 1979. Against this background we see that the estimate found here for the Netherlands, of at most around 15 % in 1980, lies in the vicinity of those obtained for Canada and the United Kingdom. For 1978 the estimate obtained in this article comes out lower for nearly all variants than the figure of nearly 10 % found by Frey for the Netherlands. It must be kept in mind that Frey uses a broader definiton than the present study.

Frey and Weck's (1983) survey makes it possible to group the countries considered according to the size of their informal economies. It turns out that four countries score higher than 10 % and only two lower than 5 %. For 1978 the Netherlands, together with the majority of other countries, can be found in the large middle category, scoring between 5 % and 10 %. Frey's percentages, incidentally, resemble educated guesses rather than empirically constructed estimates such as those attempted here.

As for the method of estimation, a survey of the literature shows that the transactions method has been applied least. This is presumably connected with the heavy demands made by this method on the collection of data. Gutmann's currency-ratio-method and the Tanzi method, which are both based on published monetary series, are used most of all. Frequent use is also made of the discrepancy method, which is based mainly on the National Accounts. It is remarkable that estimates based on this method generally turn out to be lower than those founded on the other methods (see Appendix VI for details on the literature considered).

7 Summary and conclusions

In the foregoing an attempt was made to measure the size of the informal economy in the Netherlands for the period 1965-1982 by means of Feige's transactions method. This method presupposes a normal, constant ratio of the total amount of transactions PT to national income Y, with PT equalling the total of all payments MV. Insofar as the observed ratio MV/Y exceeds the ratio considered normal, this is attributed wholly to informal transactions, which are included in MV owing to the fact that they are effected by payment. The size of the informal economy – defined as non-registered GNP – can then be calculated from the discrepancy observed.

Developments in cash payments, the first component of MV, have been estimated with the aid of a series of index numbers which were derived from developments in the circulation and lifetime of various denominations. The (absolute) volume of cash payments in the base year 1980 has been calculated from cash withdrawals, assuming a cash loop – the number of net payments between withdrawal and deposit – of 2. The estimated volume of cash payments rises over the observation period from Fl. 100 billion to Fl. 350 billion.

Transfers, the second component of MV, which are necessary for the determination of MV, have been derived from figures supplied by the four large banks and the giro services. In general, figures on bank transfers are only available as of 1971. The unknown transfers in the years 1965-1970 have been derived from the banks' demand deposits with the aid of estimated relationships. According to these estimations, total transfers in the Netherlands, which were obtained through amplification and supplementation, increased sixfold in the period 1965-1982, from Fl. 400 billion to Fl. 2.400 billion.

By way of a summary, Charts 2a and 2b show the developments of the informal economy according to the orthodox transactions method and the transactions variant attempted in section 5.4, respectively.

The curves in Chart 2a show the estimates of the informal economy on the basis of the ratio of total payments MV, estimated with alternative assumptions, to registered GNP. Each curve corresponds with one of the alternatives considered in section 5. The Charts assume throughout that the minimum size can be put at 0 %. The curves show that, viewed over time, nearly all alternatives show trough-like movements, with a minimum in 1976. The question arises whether such trough-like movements are a logical development. It is clearly an unexpected result, which is, however, a consequence of Feige's transactions method. On the other hand, the outcome obtained does not mean that the size of the informal economy, measured in billions of guil-

Chart 2a
Estimates of the informal economy on the basis of total payments MV and GNP, 1965-1982 (% of GNP)

Chart 2b
Estimates of the informal economy on the basis of total payments MV and transactions ΣT_r, 1965-1982 (% of GNP)

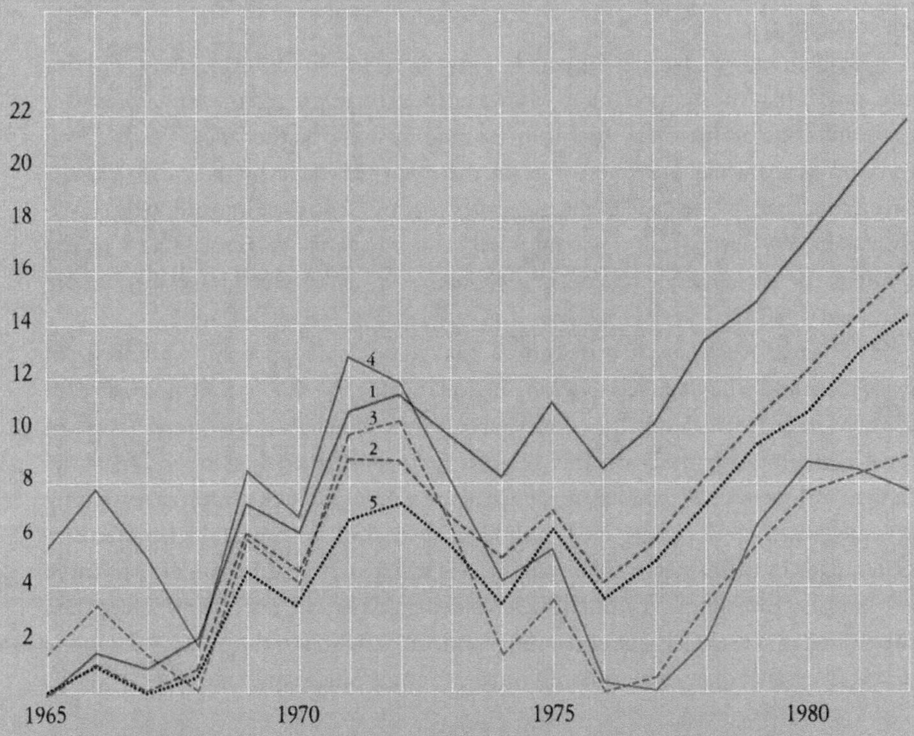

* *Explanatory note:*
The numbers shown at the curves correspond with the relevant variants given in Table 9.

ders, shows the same pattern. The growth of registered GNP is also a determining factor. On those grounds the possibility of a relative decline in the informal economy must not be excluded, especially in periods of a major expansion of GNP in nominal terms largely caused by inflation. Nevertheless there are several reasons to assume that the estimates, notably for the first period, present a distorted picture. The main reason is that as a consequence of structural changes within the Netherlands economy, it has presumably been wrongly assumed that there is a constant ratio of the value of total transactions to GNP, as the ratio of total current transactions, ΣT_r to GNP turns out to have declined by an average of 1.1 % in the years 1965-1976. From 1977 onward it has been fairly constant. The result is that the orthodox transactions method, which is based on a constant ratio of total transactions MV to GNP, has presumably distorted the estimated size of the informal economy to no mean degree for the first period. In order to eliminate this distortion to some extent the transaction method was applied in section 5.4, with the relationship $MV/\Sigma T_r$ instead of MV/Y. According to the resulting estimates (see Table 7) the relative size of the informal economy has increased steadily to 20 % of GNP in 1982 (on the basis of 0 % in 1965). Adjustment of total transactions MV for various non-current transactions yields a considerably smaller increase, to Fl. 28 billion. At the same time, the minimum consequently moves to 1976 and the trough-like movements return to some extent (Chart 2b). However, this is possibly partly due to the very tentative nature of the estimates of the non-current transactions – notably where short-term developments are concerned.

Finally, it may be asked what conclusions can be drawn from this study. The *first conclusion* is that the method followed does not lead to a clear and unequivocal answer to the question of the size of the informal economy in the Netherlands. This is due to three problems which are inherent in the method used: the assumed parallelism between total transactions and GNP, the wide variation in ways of measuring total payments and the need to allow the informal economy to fall to zero. Table 9 gives a summary of the consequences of these problems for 1976, which is usually the base year, and 1980.

The *second conclusion* of this study is that, despite the apparent weaknesses of Feige's method when applied to a long period of time the size of the informal economy in the Netherlands is considerable. This highlights the importance of further quantitative study on this subject. Comparative analysis of the literature shows, and this is the *third conclusion*, that the estimates of the informal economy obtained with Feige's transactions method virtually always come out higher than estimates made by other means. This warrants the suspicion that the estimates presented here are also overstated. A *fourth conclusion* is that, when the uncertainties regarding the estimated size are left out of consideration, all estimates in this study point in the direction of an expansion of the informal economy since the mid-1970s.

Table 9
Summary of estimates of the informal economy
(% of GNP)

Variant	On the basis of total payments MV and GNP		On the basis of total payments MV and current transactions ΣT_r	
	1976	1980	1976	1980
1. Base	0	10.1	8.7	17.5
2. Excluding income transfers	0	9.7	4.2	12.3
3. Excluding transfers to savings accounts etc.	0.7	10.2	0	7.5
4. Excluding other capital transactions	1.4	12.1	0.2	8.8
5. With alternative amplification	0	8.7	3.6	10.7
6. Base with a cash loop of 1½ instead of 2	0	10.2		
7. At constant lifetime per denomination	0	9.3		
8. On the basis of cash payments only, with a cash loop of 2	0	6.3		
9. Base with a minimum of 5% instead of 0%	5	15.6		

The *fifth conclusion* relates to a side result of this study and concerns the velocity of circulation of notes and coin and of demand deposits. According to the estimation results the velocity of circulation of notes and coin increased from nearly 13½ to over 15½ in the period 1965-1982. The estimates of transfers indicate that the velocity of circulation of demand deposits has presumably increased much less sharply than is generally assumed. The estimated transfers (including non-financial transactions with foreign countries) yield an increase in the velocity of circulation of demand deposits from 43 to nearly 46. This relatively slight rise is presumably the result of the fact that the increase in the velocity of circulation of business sector deposits has been largely undone by the strong growth of the share of personal sector deposits, which have a much lower velocity of circulation, of around 12 (including cash withdrawals)[23].

Despite this comparatively small rise in the velocity of circulation of currency and demand deposits taken separately, money (M_1) as a whole saw its velocity of circulation undergo a remarkable increase from 29 in 1965 to over 36 in 1982. This is for the greater part due to the fact that payments are increasingly effected in the form of

[23] In these calculations, debit positions were left out of consideration, while total debits were included in the estimated totals. The velocity of circulation of demand deposits will therefore be lower in reality, and will presumably have increased (even more) slowly.

transfers. It needs no elaboration that notably this last conclusion about the velocity of circulation of currency and demand deposits pertains to monetary analysis which is incidentally also the basic starting point of the transactions method applied in this study.

Appendix

Appendix I. Estimation of cash payments with the lifetime method

Following Laurent (1970) it was assumed that on average G payments are made with a banknote of denomination i before it becomes unfit for further circulation. This implies that, at a lifetime of L_t^i years during period t, on average G/L_t^i payments are made every year with banknotes of denomination i.

The average lifetime in years of the various denominations can be estimated with the aid of the so-called circulation formula [1].

$$L_t^i = \frac{\overline{C}_t^i}{\frac{1}{2}(A_t^i + N_t^i)} = \frac{\overline{C}_t^i}{A_t^i + \frac{1}{2}(N_t^i - A_t^i)} = \frac{\overline{C}_t^i}{A_t^i + \frac{1}{2}\Delta C_t^i} \qquad (1)$$

with $\overline{C}_t^i$ the average number of banknotes in circulation and A_t^i en N_t^i the numbers of rejected and newly issued banknotes of denomination i in year t. The number of newly issued banknotes N_t in year t is not known for the entire observation period. The expansion of the circulation $N_t - A_t$ can, however, be approximated by the increase in the circulation ΔC_t. The circulation formula then becomes the right hand term in equation (1).

As can be seen in the first five columns of Table I - A, the lifetime series calculated by means of this formula shows a rather erratic development in the short term. The main reason for this is to be found in the policy pursued by the Netherlands Bank with regard to the sorting, withdrawal and issue of banknotes. Adjustments should therefore be made as much as possible for changes in the calculated lifetime as a result of such external factors. For this reason short-term fluctuations have been eliminated by determining a trend for the lifetime of each denomination with the aid of regression, and by subsequently calculating the lifetime according to this trend (last five columns of Table I - A). For the four smallest denominations the average lifetime decreases in time, be it that the decrease is small for the 100-guilder note. In the case of the 1000-guilder note, the lifetime increases.

---

[1] This formula was used, by among others, Den Butter and Coenen (1981). On the basis of the first member, the total number of payments with denomination i in year t ($B_t^i = \overline{C}_t^i \cdot G/L_t^i$) yields the formula $\frac{1}{2}G(A_t^i + N_t^i)$. This is the same formula as that ultimately used by Laurent, albeit that he derived it in a somewhat different manner.

Table I - A
Average lifetime per denomination, 1965-1982
(in years)

	Calculated with circulation formula					Calculated with trend equations [1]				
	Fl. 5	Fl. 10	Fl. 25	Fl. 100	Fl. 1000	Fl. 5	Fl. 10	Fl. 25	Fl. 100	Fl. 1000
1965	-	1.59	1.95	2.77	2.24	-	1.61	1.90	2.95	2.28
1966	-	1.57	1.93	3.17	2.28	-	1.57	1.83	2.93	2.33
1967	1.40	1.64	1.98	3.37	2.63	1.28	1.53	1.77	2.91	2.38
1968	1.63	1.53	1.70	2.89	2.30	1.26	1.49	1.71	2.89	2.44
1969	1.22	1.53	1.55	3.01	2.62	1.23	1.45	1.65	2.87	2.49
1970	1.07	1.44	1.43	2.65	2.33	1.20	1.41	1.59	2.85	2.54
1971	1.07	1.40	1.40	2.67	2.52	1.18	1.37	1.53	2.83	2.59
1972	1.08	1.19	1.25	2.28	3.02	1.15	1.33	1.46	2.81	2.64
1973	1.02	1.39	1.01	1.44	1.67	1.12	1.29	1.40	2.79	2.69
1974	1.00	1.09	2.07	3.51	3.24	1.10	1.25	1.34	2.77	2.74
1975	0.95	1.03	1.25	4.11	3.46	1.07	1.21	1.28	2.75	2.79
1976	0.94	1.02	1.09	2.81	2.96	1.04	1.17	1.22	2.73	2.84
1977	0.92	1.13	1.13	2.41	2.21	1.02	1.13	1.15	2.71	2.89
1978	0.90	0.97	1.03	2.32	3.10	0.99	1.09	1.09	2.69	2.94
1979	0.95	1.17	0.98	2.32	4.32	0.96	1.05	1.03	2.67	2.99
1980	0.95	1.00	1.00	2.27	4.67	0.94	1.01	0.97	2.65	3.04
1981	1.31	1.20	1.06	3.42	5.73	0.91	0.97	0.91	2.63	3.09
1982	1.08	1.11	1.00	2.13	2.79	0.88	0.93	0.84	2.61	3.14

[1] The trend equations were estimated for the period 1965-1981, except that for the 5-guilder note. In the case of the 1000-guilder note, the years 1979-1981 were left out of consideration in connection with marked outliers.

From the resulting lifetime series, a series expressed in terms of G was calculated for cash payments in year t, MVC_t:

$$MVC_t = \sum_i^5 MVC_t^i = G \cdot \sum_i^5 w_i \cdot \overline{C}_t^i / L_t^i \qquad (2)$$

with MVC_t^i cash payments with denomination i in the year t, w_i the nominal value of denomination i, $\overline{C}_t^i$ the average number of banknotes in circulation of denomination i in year t (see Table I - B) and L_t^i the trend lifetime of denomination i in year t. It follows from the line of thought pursued that 1980 saw cash payments of Fl. 9.34 billion. By equating this figure with the total transactions calculated for that year by means of the cash loop method, viz. Fl. 320.4 billion (Table I - C, first column), G is found to have a value of over 34. With this choice for parameter G, total cash payments in guilders in the other years have been determined (second column in Table I - C).

The value of 34 found for G is considerably smaller than the 129 estimated by Laurent via another method for the United States [2]. As the average lifetime of banknotes in the Netherlands is much shorter than that in the United States, the outcomes for the

Table I-B
Composition of the banknote circulation, 1965-1982
(annual averages, in thousands)

	Fl. 5	Fl. 10	Fl. 25	Fl. 100	Fl. 1000	Total
1965	–	64,010	46,600	41,167	1,174	152,951
1966	–	65,110	46,860	46,150	1,281	159,401
1967	9,640	62,650	45,884	48,978	1,372	168,524
1968	14,720	60,880	45,388	49,979	1,500	172,467
1969	18,100	60,810	46,496	56,239	1,675	183,320
1970	20,840	60,280	47,424	55,144	1,844	185,532
1971	22,860	60,700	48,388	58,034	2,037	192,019
1972	24,000	59,630	49,520	61,759	2,353	197,262
1973	25,940	60,910	52,796	66,016	2,715	208,377
1974	28,020	60,710	55,440	70,529	3,042	217,741
1975	30,400	60,650	57,468	77,094	3,493	229,105
1976	33,700	61,810	61,312	89,902	3,902	250,626
1977	36,220	62,370	63,808	99,420	4,179	265,997
1978	38,660	63,240	68,052	106,651	4,665	281,268
1979	41,840	64,260	71,108	113,476	5,173	295,857
1980	45,460	65,680	73,836	121,055	5,993	312,024
1981	47,983	66,636	78,400	121,411	6,411	320,841
1982	48,299	65,569	79,738	121,243	7,025	321,874

Explanatory note:
The circulation of the Fl. 50 banknote introduced in September 1982 has been equally distributed over the Fl. 25 and Fl. 100 banknotes.

annual number of payments per denomination are very similar for the two countries. Laurent's G of 129 means, for example, that in 1967 on average 12 payments were made with a $ 100 banknote. The G of over 34 found here implies that in that same year the Fl. 100 banknote was also used for, on average, 12 payments.

The third column of Table I-C shows cash payments on the assumption that the lifetime is constant per denomination and equal to the average value assumed during the observation period. The increase over the observation period is consequently

[2] For G, Laurent takes the value for which total transactions MV, i.e. the (known) transfers plus (known) cash payments, except for G, has a maximum correlation with GNP over the period 1875-1967. For such a calculation of the correlation, the observation period considered here seems too short. Another objection to this approach – certainly in this context – is that G follows from correlation calculations between MV and observed GNP, instead of the (unknown) total, i.e. observed and unobserved GNP.

substantially smaller (182 % instead of 242 %), lagging slightly behind the growth of the circulation of notes and coin in this period, which came out at over 200 %. The latter is the result of a gradual shift from banknotes with a smaller denomination and a relatively short lifetime or a higher intensity of use to larger denominations with a relatively long lifetime or a low intensity of use, which is connected with the income elasticity per denomination [cf. Fase and Van Nieuwkerk (1976, 1977)].

Table I-C
Estimated cash payments, 1965-1982
(billions of guilders)

	Cash loop method	Lifetime method with G=34.3	Lifetime method with constant lifetime [1] and G=37.0	Lifetime method with constant lifetime equal for all denominations [2]	On the basis of Uyttewaal's index numbers
1965	60.0	102.5	120.2	113.9	–
1966	65.8	109.0	128.9	125.2	–
1967	74.2	115.0	134.2	132.4	–
1968	86.0	119.3	137.3	134.4	103.6
1969	103.2	131.5	149.4	140.4	120.6
1970	120.7	134.6	151.2	147.0	126.1
1971	141.1	143.1	158.9	155.5	143.2
1972	161.5	154.0	168.9	169.3	149.3
1973	179.8	168.3	182.5	180.9	158.4
1974	195.0	182.0	195.2	191.5	–
1975	216.2	199.8	212.0	208.7	–
1976	237.0	227.1	238.2	234.0	215.2
1977	259.5	248.0	256.9	256.3	247.4
1978	273.2	270.5	276.9	277.5	287.5
1979	297.4	292.8	295.9	296.5	292.8
1980	320.4	320.4	320.4	320.4	–
1981	331.1	336.3	330.5	331.9	–
1982	346.5	350.7	339.6	343.0	–

[1] The lifetime has been equated per denomination with its average value in the observation period considered for the adjustment of the trend equations.

[2] At a constant relationship of 15.3 between cash payments and average circulation of notes and coin.

In the fourth column the lifetime has not only been assumed to be constant, but also equal for all denominations. The estimated payments are then proportional to the circulation of currency. It consequently also rises by over 200 %, thus coming out at a level which lies between the two other variants. The last column of Table I-C gives the results which follow from the index numbers calculated earlier by Uyttewaal (1981) via an analogous method. These are based on un-smoothed lifetime figures. They consequently show a much more erratic pattern and are not very well comparable with the figures in the second column, apart even from the shorter, interrupted observation period.

Appendix II. The giro transfer system

The fragmentary registration of transfers (including guaranteed cheque payments) is partly due to the typical structure of the Netherlands payments system. There are three giro circuits, viz. that of the Netherlands Bank, that of the banking system and that of the Postal Cheque and Giro Services/Post Office Savings Bank also comprising the *Municipal Giro Service of Amsterdam* since 1979. Figure II - A shows a diagram of the various payment flows within and between these three giro systems.

The giro system of the *Netherlands Bank*, where the banks, the Banks' Clearing Institution and the Postal Cheque and Giro Services/Post Office Savings Bank hold one or more accounts, processes, first of all, payments between the other two giro systems and interbank transfers (including settlement). In addition, it processes transfers to and from and between the various other account holders of the Netherlands Bank [3]. These also include payments to and from the Treasury, as well as a small part of transfers to and from other countries, insofar as these are settled via foreign central banks. The bulk of the banks' external payments, however, takes place direct via their correspondents or via accounts held at these banks by foreign banks.

In the giro circuits of the *banking system* a distinction can be made between intrabank and interbank transfers. Intrabank transfers are transfers between account holders of one banking institution. These are still mostly processed internally (A), but processing by the Banks' Clearing Institution (BCI) – as in the case of guaranteed cheques is also possible (B). The banks' interbank transfers relate to transfers between account holders of different banks. The majority of these transfers (in numbers), estimated to be over 98 % in 1982, are processed by the BCI (C). Eventual settlement takes place via the settlement account of the BCI and the accounts held by the banks concerned at the Netherlands Bank (C ´). In addition, direct transfers are effected between the banks (H); settlement of these transfers takes place via their accounts at the Netherlands Bank. Generally speaking, these involve very large amounts.

The giro circuit of the Postal Cheque and Giro Services comprises all postal giro account holders. These include the public authorities, the banks (including the Netherlands Bank) and the Banks' Clearing Institution. This circuit processes giro transfers from one postal giro account to another (F), which include transfers from postal giro accounts to bank giro accounts and vice versa (G and E). These transfers

[3] The other 640-odd institutions holding an account at the Netherlands Bank, next to the banks (370), the Banks' Clearing Institution, the Postal Cheque and Giro Services and the central government (9) include 71 foreign central banks, the local authorities, ecclasiastical, cultural and social institutions, security brokers, pension funds, social insurance funds, savings banks, various associations for trade and industry, and a number of large firms.

Chart IIa
Diagram of giro payments in the Netherlands

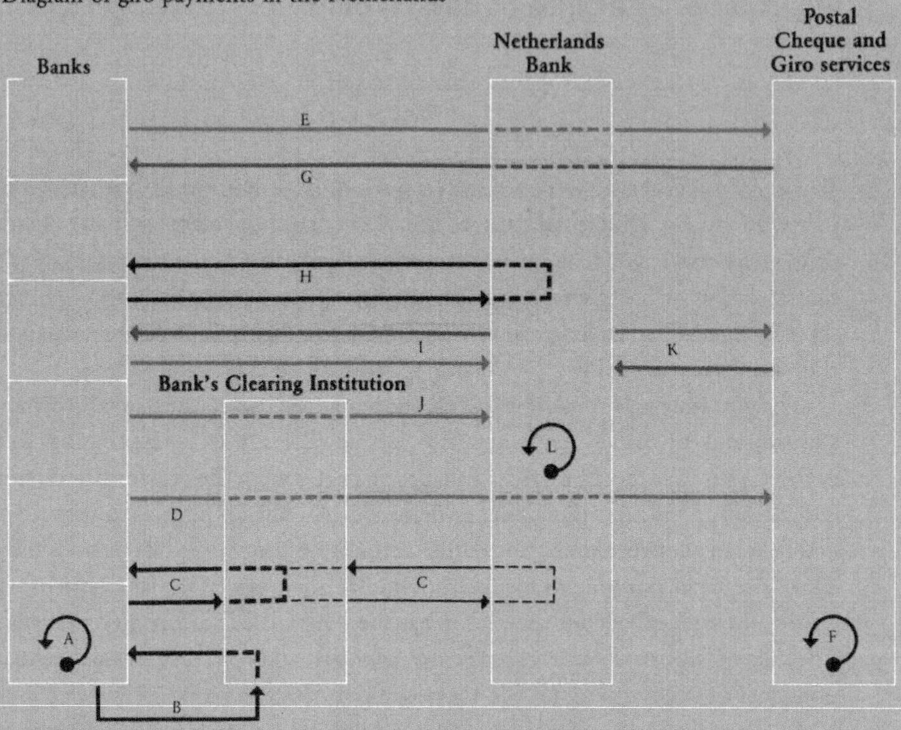

Explanatory note:
A – Intrabank transfers
B – Intrabank transfers via BCI
C – Interbank transactions via BCI (and the BCI-settlement account at the Netherlands Bank)
D – Transfers from banks to Postal Cheque and Giro Services via BCI (and the Netherlands Bank)
E – Transfers from banks to Postal Cheque and Giro Services via the Netherlands Bank
F – Transfers between account holders of Postal Cheque and Giro Services
G – Transfers from Postal Cheque and Giro Services to banks via the Netherlands Bank
H – Interbank transfers via the Netherlands Bank
I – Direct transfers from banks to the Netherlands Bank (including Treasury) and vice versa
J – Transfers from banks to the Netherlands Bank (including Treasury) via BCI and vice versa
K – Transfers from Postal Cheque and Giro Services to the Netherlands Bank (including Treasury) and vice versa
L – Other transfers between account holders of the Netherlands Bank

are effected, in the first instance, via the postal giro account of the bank concerned or of the Banks' Clearing Institution. Transfers between the two systems are marked by a certain degree of asymmetry. The banks' transfers to the Postal Cheque and Giro Services go partly via the Banks' Clearing Institution (D) and partly (notably the large amounts) direct via their account at the Netherlands Bank and their postal giro accounts (E). However, transfers in the other direction are effected entirely – or almost entirely – via the banks' postal giro accounts and subsequently via the Netherlands Bank (G). In principle, only the balance of payment flows E and G need pass the Netherlands Bank.

Appendix III. Amplification of bank transfers

The estimates of transfers at banks are based on data on debits supplied by the four major banks, i.e. ABN, Amro-bank, NMB and Rabo-bank. The share of these institutions in total demand deposits held at the banking system came to an average of 83 % in the observation period 1965-1982.

Debits at the other banks which have not, in the first instance, been taken into consideration here, were estimated by multiplying the demand deposits outstanding

Table III - A
Estimation of missing transfers, 1965-1982
(amounts in billions of guilders)

	Demand deposits		Velocity of circulation of demand deposits		Unknown transfers	
	total banks	of which unobserved banks	representative bank	average at banks observed	at velocity of circulation of representative bank [1]	at average velocity of circulation [2]
1965	6.1	1.3	31.1	41.8	40.9	55.0
1966	6.4	1.3	35.3	44.6	45.9	57.8
1967	6.9	1.4	35.6	43.2	48.9	59.3
1968	8.2	1.6	36.4	41.4	59.0	67.1
1969	9.3	1.8	42.0	43.4	77.6	80.1
1970	10.4	1.7	43.9	44.0	74.8	75.0
1971	13.0	2.2	45.6	41.3	102.5	92.8
1972	16.4	3.1	39.7	36.7	123.5	114.0
1973	17.1	3.0	43.3	39.0	129.5	116.7
1974	16.7	2.4	54.9	44.9	133.5	109.3
1975	21.2	3.4	47.4	40.0	163.1	137.4
1976	23.5	3.4	48.9	39.4	164.3	132.5
1977	27.9	4.1	46.4	36.7	190.3	150.3
1978	28.3	4.0	54.2	40.0	215.5	159.1
1979	28.2	4.2	56.6	43.7	237.5	183.2
1980	28.6	4.3	63.6	46.0	273.5	197.9
1981	29.4	4.2	67.1	48.1	282.0	202.1
1982	31.8	4.6	67.2	46.6	310.2	215.2

1 Product of second and third column.

2 Product of second and fourth column.

at these banks, which are reported to the Netherlands Bank, by a relevant velocity of circulation of demand deposits. We therefore took the velocity of circulation recorded at one of the banks considered, which in our opinion most resembles that of the unknown part of the banking system. This velocity of circulation can be found in the third column of Table III - A. The fifth column gives the resulting totals for the banks which are not included in this study. Unless stated otherwise, these estimates were used to construct the series for total transfers. The estimated debits at the other banks, not being one of the group of four major banks, increased by over 650 % in the period 1965-1982, from over Fl. 40 billion to Fl. 310 billion (fifth column). In that same period debits at the banks considered, which are, incidentally, not separately mentioned in Table 3 of the main text, increased by 540 %, from Fl. 200 billion to Fl. 1,270 billion.

This amplification is based on far-reaching assumptions. For example, no account is taken of debit positions, while the velocity of circulation of demand deposits at the banks not considered is equated *a priori* with that of one of the observed banking institutions. In order to be able to study the sensitivity of the estimation results to this latter assumption in greater detail an alternative amplification was also applied. This meant that on the basis of the average velocity of circulation of demand deposits at all banks considered, a calculation was made of transaction totals at the banks not considered (the last column in Table III - A). As the velocity of circulation shows a much smaller rise the resulting debits increased considerably less, viz. by 290 %, than when the basis is a velocity of circulation recorded at one bank considered representative.

Appendix IV. Comparison with transactions as estimated by Cramer

This appendix compares the estimates, presented in the main text, of transactions in the years 1965-1982 with those made by Cramer (1981a), which relate to 1974-1978. The comparison concerns only those years which the two studies have in common, viz. 1974-1978. Table IV-A gives both estimates and their components for this period.

Table IV - A
Comparison of estimated payments, 1974-1978
(amounts in billions of guilders)

		1974	1975	1976	1977	1978
Cash payments						
	E	182.0	199.8	227.1	248.0	270.5
	C	178.2	212.9	241.4	265.3	283.9
	(E - C in % of C)	(2)	(-6)	(-6)	(-7)	(-5)
Transfers						
Giro services	E	226.8	248.7	276.8	284.0	295.3
	C	246.7	284.2	316.5	327.2	348.9
	(E - C in % of C)	(-8)	(-13)	(-13)	(-13)	(-15)
Banks	E	780.0	878.3	965.8	1073.8	1199.6
	C	326.1	388.6	453.4	523.8	578.5
	(E - C in % of C)	(139)	(126)	(113)	(105)	(107)
Central Government	E	55.8	68.5	80.7	89.2	103.6
	C	49.2	60.9	72.7	79.9	95.6
	(E - C in % of C)	(13)	(12)	(11)	(12)	(8)
Total						
	E	1244.6	1395.3	1550.4	1695.0	1869.0
	C	800.2	946.6	1084.0	1196.2	1306.9
	(E - C in % of C)	(56)	(47)	(43)	(42)	(43)

Explanatory note:
E: estimate; C: Cramer's estimate.
For comparability's sake, transfers from foreign exchange and savings accounts to giro accounts, as estimated by Cramer, and the 'other payments', which together made up 2.5% of total payments in 1978, were left out of consideration.

Cash payments

Both studies base the estimation of cash payments on cash withdrawals and a cash loop of 2. In the present study, however, cash payments were estimated in this way only for the base year 1980. From this estimate, figures for the other years were subsequently derived with the aid of index numbers. Cramer, on the other hand, calculates cash payments for all five years considered from cash withdrawals, which are known for the giro services and which he calculates for the banks from the demand deposits held there, assuming a withdrawal frequency of 4. According to estimates obtained here, the withdrawal frequency at the banks (in 1978) came to no more than 3.1, which means that Cramer overestimates cash withdrawals. However, owing to the fact that cash withdrawals from checking accounts at savings banks and from savings accounts and time deposits are also taken into consideration, both estimates correspond fairly well [4].

Transfers

Total transfers found here for the giro services turn out to be much lower than that found by Cramer. The difference between the two is mainly due to the fact that there are major differences in three basic starting points. First, transfers from the central government are regarded as part of the central government's transfers and not as part of the giro services' transfers; secondly, there are deviations in the manner in which allowance is made for double counting, and finally there is the fact that, contrary to Cramer's approach, cash withdrawals from accounts held by someone else are regarded as payments in this study. According to the estimates thus obtained transfers at the giro services in the period observed increased somewhat less rapidly than according to Cramer's findings.

Transfers at banks and savings banks – even excluding transfers to other countries – total more than twice the estimate made by Cramer for the banks. As his estimates have been derived from figures supplied by the Banks' Clearing Institution, and the transfers estimated here are based on figures compiled by the banks, they cannot be compared in great detail. Cramer has presumably underestimated the volume of payments taking place outside the Banks' Clearing Institution, especially intrabank transfers. The faster increase in his estimates can be explained by the fact that these are based on figures recorded at this Institution, which certainly grew much faster in the early years than total transfers.

---

4 If cash withdrawals at savings banks are also taken into account, the cash loop will *ceteris paribus* be lower than when they are left out of consideration, as in Cramers study. The cash loop used here is therefore not wholly comparable with that used by Cramer.

The estimates of the central government's transfers differ because, in the present study, imports by the public authorities are not included in the central government's transfers, whereas that part of central government payments which runs via the giro services – and which Cramer regards as giro service transfers – is.

Appendix V. Estimation of total transactions

The total amount of transactions can be estimated, not only from the payments side, but also from the transactions side. This was done earlier by Niesten (1968), Jonker (1973) and Cramer (1981a). Their estimates can, in principle, be useful to us in achieving our goal. The main sources of data of these researchers were the publications of the Central Bureau of Statistics (CBS). In order to bring the series up to date and because, within the framework of this study, a number of transactions require different treatment, the transaction total was estimated anew for the years 1965-1982. The estimation, which is no more than a very rough approximation, is elaborated in greater detail with the aid of three categories of transactions.

Current transactions

Current transactions ΣT_r include transactions which are directly connected with output. In view of the availability of data this transactions category has been approximated in terms of receipts. By adding the net external payments, an estimate was subsequently obtained of the payments which corresponds with debits estimated on the basis of monetary figures. The series used are shown in Table V - A. Insofar as they stem from the National Accounts (NA), the numbers of the relevant table and item are added.

The turnover of the retail trade has been derived from consumer spending (NA Table 43), excluding housing services, public authority services, services relating to transportation and health care, and the services of banks, assurance companies and social institutions. This turnover also comprises the sales of the retail trade, so that, if double counting is to be avoided, these should be excluded from industrial sales. For the estimation of the turnover of the wholesale trade, use was made of index numbers supplied in Table I of the Statistisch Zakboek (Statistical Digest) published by the CBS. On the basis of the results of the Algemene Groothandelstelling 1967 (General Wholesale Census) made by the CBS, the wholesale turnover rates of the various sectors have been calculated for the period 1965-1982. For the sectors for which no or only limited index numbers are available, it has been assumed that their wholesale turnover has undergone a development which corresponds with their sales as published in the National Accounts. As is the case with the sales of the retail trade, the sales of the wholesale trade should also be eliminated from the total sales of industry. In conformity with Cramer's approach, the output of the public authorities was approximated by regarding part of the income transfers to the public authorities which are to be estimated in the following paragraphs, as payments for public authority output. These have been calculated as the total goods and services supplied to the public authorities and the services of the factors of production.

A number of payments within the sectors distinguished by the CBS are not contained in the total current transactions thus obtained. These include payments between the business sector and the banking system, such as the personal sector's interest payments on mortgages. It appears from the new classification of the National Accounts that in 1981 these payments involved an approximated amount of Fl. 75 billion, i.e. some 6% of the estimated total. On the other hand, the estimated total does include transactions which do not actually involve payments. This is the case for, among others, housing services, included in industrial sales, insofar as they relate to home ownership. The estimates obtained here are, on average around 10% higher than Cramer's, although their increase over the years 1965-1977 turns out to be virtually the same (235% against 250%). As Cramer does not give a more detailed breakdown, the discrepancy cannot be analysed.

Income transfers

Table V - B gives an estimation of income transfers. Social insurance paid statistically, but not in reality to the personal sector has been left out of account, because it is already included in the social insurance contributions paid by the business sector. For a similar reason the wage tax already deducted has been excluded from income transfers. The output of the public authorities estimated in the previous section has been deducted from the resulting total amount. The results obtained barely deviate from Cramer's estimates.

In the case of income transfers, too, the estimated transactions totals are no more than very rough approximations of payments which have actually taken place. These approximations are presumably underestimated. A major part of income transfers, for example, involve several giro transfers. Likewise, indirect tax payments – which are partly refunded – will be higher than the net result given here.

Capital transactions

To obtain estimates of capital transactions (Table V - C) which are even more tentative in character, use has been made of various publications. Repayments on mortgages have been calculated from the difference between gross mortgage lending as reported by the CBS and net mortgage lending as it follows from changes in the positions shown in the Netherlands Bank's Annual Report. The other items are self-evident. The estimates obtained turn out to be considerably lower than Cramer's. This is to a major extent the result of the fact that he considers deposits into and withdrawals from savings accounts (in 1978 Fl. 88 billion) as capital transactions. If these had been included, the transactions total estimated here would be 16 % and 5 % higher in 1965 and 1978 respectively.

Table V–A
Current transactions, 1965-1982
(billions of guilders)

	NA	1965	1966	1967	1968	1969
1. Industrial sales (output minus increase in stocks)	27.1-16.8	124.5	135.0	145.4	160.8	171.1
Minus:						
1a. Sales of wholesale and retail trade	28.61/66	15.1	16.2	17.7	19.4	19.1
1b. Sales of assurance companies	28.82	1.6	1.8	2.0	2.3	2.7
2. Turnover retail trade	43	33.4	35.6	38.1	41.2	46.0
3. Turnover wholesale trade		63.0	66.4	70.0	75.8	82.9
4. Re-exports	52.A3	0.7	0.8	1.0	1.2	1.4
5. Investment income of life assurance companies	48.8	0.6	0.7	0.8	0.9	1.0
6. Investment income of pension funds	48.8	0.8	1.0	1.2	1.4	1.7
7. Public authority income from participations and investment	2.2.52/53	1.0	1.1	1.2	1.5	1.8
8. Investment income of social insurance funds	3.2.52-54	0.2	0.2	0.2	0.2	0.2
9. Personal sector income from investment and business activities	4.2.58/60	14.3	14.1	15.6	16.4	17.8
10. Goods and services supplied by the public authorities	2.1.51-54	0.5	0.6	0.6	0.7	0.8
11. Wages and salaries to the personal sector	4.2.51-54	30.7	33.9	36.6	39.8	45.9
12. 'Output' of public authorities		13.4	14.9	16.8	18.5	20.8
of which:						
a. Delivery of goods and services to public authorities by industry	2.1.01	5.5	6.1	6.9	7.8	8.4
b. Delivery of goods and services to public authorities by foreign countries	2.1.02	0.6	0.5	0.6	0.6	0.7
c. Services of factors of production	2.1.04	7.3	8.3	9.3	10.2	11.7
13. Net payments to foreign countries (goods, services, income)	51.15/18-51.3/6	-0.3	0.5	-0.1	-0.6	2.8
Total [1 – 1a – 1b + 2 inclusive to 13]		266.0	286.7	307.6	336.1	372.5
Ditto, corrected for 1977 revision of National Accounts[b]		275.8	296.9	318.7	348.1	385.8
Cramer's estimate (1981a)		241.2	261.1	279.8	306.7	342.4

[a] Provisional or estimated figure.

[b] Calculated as the sum total of the separate components adjusted, where necessary, for breaks in series.

1970	1971	1972	1973	1974	1975	1976	1977	1977	1978	1979	1980	1981	1982
194.8	214.9	236.7	272.4	324.2	346.3	395.0	424.2	437.7	464.6	511.0	560.1	604.4	618.7
22.4	23.9	26.3	29.6	35.7	37.7	42.3	46.7	51.3	55.5	59.9	62.7	61.4	62.9
3.0	3.4	3.8	4.4	4.9	5.1	5.9	6.7	6.4	7.5	8.4	9.2	9.9	10.2
51.8	57.6	63.3	70.7	78.7	89.2	101.6	111.8	119.8	128.5	136.6	144.6	148.8	152.7
93.9	102.5	110.8	126.0	143.6	150.6	168.7	177.4	177.4	185.4	197.6	212.0	218.9[a]	217.0[a]
2.1	2.7	3.1	4.4	4.6	5.8	6.8	6.5	6.8	6.9	8.5	11.4	13.4	13.7
1.1	1.3	1.4	1.6	1.9	2.4	2.9	3.4	3.4	3.8	4.3	4.8	5.4	6.0
2.0	2.5	3.0	3.5	4.4	5.5	6.6	7.8	7.8	9.0	10.5	12.3	14.5	16.6
2.2	2.2	2.7	3.1	4.2	6.8	9.4	10.9	10.9	10.9	12.8	15.9	20.6	21.4
0.3	0.3	0.3	0.4	0.6	0.6	0.7	0.7	0.7	0.8	1.0	1.0	0.9	0.8
18.3	19.7	22.2	26.1	26.0	22.8	28.7	27.5	33.5	36.4	36.1	36.5	39.4	43.5
0.8	1.0	1.1	1.3	1.6	1.7	2.0	2.3	2.4	2.7	2.8	3.1	3.3	3.5
52.5	59.8	66.8	75.6	87.0	98.6	109.0	119.5	123.5	133.9	143.4	152.1	155.2	160.7
23.6	27.5	30.2	33.1	38.8	44.9	51.4	55.4	56.0	60.9	65.5	69.6	72.0	73.9
9.4	10.8	11.6	12.2	14.2	16.2	18.7	19.5	19.5	21.0	22.3	24.0	25.3	25.5
1.1	1.3	0.8	0.6	0.7	0.8	1.2	1.3	1.4	1.8	2.3	2.6	2.8	3.1
13.1	15.4	17.8	20.3	24.0	27.9	31.4	34.6	35.1	38.2	40.9	42.9	43.9	45.4
1.6	0.0	-5.0	-6.9	-6.9	-7.0	-8.8	-3.8	-3.8	0.2	2.0	2.7	-11.3	-13.0
419.6	464.6	506.6	577.2	668.0	725.4	825.8	890.3	918.4	981.0	1063.6	1154.2	1204.2	1242.4
434.2	480.7	524.6	597.9	690.8	749.1	853.6	918.4	918.4	981.0	1063.6	1154.2	1204.2	1242.4
385.7	430.0	473.9	540.2	624.9	685.6	778.8	844.9	.	894.6	.	.	.	.

Table V–B
Estimated transactions total, 1965-1982
(billions of guilders)

	NA	1965	1966	1967	1968	1969
Industry:						
1. Indirect taxes	1.2.09	6.9	7.7	8.7	10.1	10.7
2. Direct taxes	1.2.11	1.9	1.9	2.1	2.5	3.2
3. Capital transfers to pension funds	1.5.02	0.2	0.2	0.3	0.4	0.4
4. Capital transfers to central government	1.5.03	0.1	0.1	0.2	0.1	0.1
Central government and other public authorities:						
5. Indirect taxes to central government	2.2.07	0.0	0.0	0.0	0.0	0.0
6. Income transfers via social insurance	2.2.10	0.5	0.5	0.5	1.0	1.0
7. Income transfers to personal sector	2.2.11	1.7	2.1	2.6	2.7	3.1
8. Income transfers via pension funds	2.2.12	0.1	0.1	0.1	0.1	0.1
9. Income transfers to foreign countries	2.2.13	0.2	0.2	0.3	0.3	0.3
10. Domestic capital transfers	2.5.01-04	0.8	0.8	0.9	1.0	1.1
11. External capital transfers	2.5.05	0.0	0.0	0.1	0.1	0.2
12. Price-reducing subsidies	38.C.8	1.2	1.2	1.3	1.4	1.6
13. Price-raising levies	38.B.2	0.7	0.7	0.6	0.6	0.5
Social insurance funds:						
14. Income transfers to personal sector	3.2.04	7.8	9.2	10.4	12.2	14.4
15. Income transfers to foreign countries	3.2.05	0.0	0.0	0.1	0.1	0.1
16. Capital transfers	3.5.01/02	–	–	0.1	0.1	0.1
Households and private non-profit institutions:						
17. Social insurance contributions	4.2.04	7.7	9.0	10.4	12.3	14.5
18. Direct taxes	4.2.03	6.9	8.1	9.4	9.6	11.3
Minus: 18a. Wage taxes	37.A.4	3.2	3.8	4.4	4.8	6.0
19. Income transfers to central government	4.2.05	0.5	0.5	0.6	0.7	0.8
20. Income transfers to foreign countries	4.2.06	0.1	0.2	0.2	0.3	0.4
21. Net life assurance premiums	4.5.01	3.2	3.8	4.2	4.6	5.1
22. Imputed life assurance premiums	4.5.02	1.4	1.7	2.0	2.3	2.7
23. Premiums to foreign pension funds	4.5.03	0.0	0.0	0.0	0.0	0.0
24. Capital transfers to central government	4.5.04	0.3	0.2	0.2	0.2	0.3
25. Indemnity insurance premiums (CBS, Stat. Zakboek, Table O19)		1.4	1.6	1.8	2.0	2.3
Life assurance companies, pension funds etc.:						
26. Supplements to pensions to personal sector	6.2.02	0.1	0.1	0.1	0.1	0.1
27. Payments to personal sector	6.5.01	1.8	2.1	2.3	2.6	2.9
28. Payments to foreign countries	6.5.02	0.0	0.1	0.1	0.1	0.1
29. Payments by indemnity insurance companies (CBS, Stat. Zakboek, Table O19)		0.7	0.9	1.0	1.2	1.3
30. Public authority 'output' (see Table 4B, item 12)		13.4	14.9	16.8	18.5	20.8
Total income transfers (1 inclusive to 29–18a–30)		29.5	34.4	39.4	45.2	51.8
Ditto, adjusted for 1977 revision of National Accounts [b]		29.4	34.3	39.2	45.1	51.7
Cramer's estimate (1981a)		30.6	35.5	41.0	47.1	54.3

[a] Provisional or estimated figure.

[b] Calculated as the sum total of the separate components adjusted, where necessary, for breaks in series.

1970	1971	1972	1973	1974	1975	1976	1977	1977	1978	1979	1980	1981	1982
13.0	15.0	17.5	19.8	21.2	23.5	27.7	32.1	32.1	35.5	37.4	40.0	40.6	41.5
3.0	3.8	4.2	5.0	5.7	7.4	7.6	8.2	8.2	8.3	8.3	10.2	11.1	11.3
0.4	0.5	0.6	0.9	0.9	1.1	1.2	1.4	1.4	1.5	1.5	1.8	1.7	2.0
0.1	0.1	0.1	0.2	0.2	0.3	1.0	0.3	0.3	0.4	0.3	0.4	0.4	0.5
0.0	0.1	0.1	0.1	0.1	0.2	0.2	0.2	0.2	0.3	0.3	0.4	0.4	0.4
1.0	1.2	1.4	1.6	1.8	3.6	5.7	5.6	5.6	8.7	9.9	11.5	9.9	7.8
3.7	4.6	5.6	7.0	8.3	11.2	13.6	14.6	14.6	15.7	16.8	17.9	21.5	26.6
0.1	0.1	0.1	0.1	0.1	0.1	0.1	0.2	0.2	0.2	0.2	0.2	0.2	0.2
0.3	1.3	1.5	1.9	1.9	3.1	3.3	4.1	4.1	4.8	5.0	5.1	5.2	5.6
1.3	1.5	1.6	2.3	2.1	3.4	4.2	2.6	2.9	6.1	5.2	8.1	9.3	9.6
0.3	0.2	0.3	0.3	0.2	0.3	0.4	0.4	0.4	0.4	0.6	0.6	0.8	0.8
2.0	1.8	2.2	3.2	3.5	3.9	6.1	6.9	6.9	7.6	8.8	9.0	8.5	9.6
0.5	0.6	0.5	0.4	0.2	0.5	1.0	1.3	1.3	1.1	0.9	0.7	0.6	0.6
16.7	20.0	23.8	27.7	33.2	39.8	45.7	51.6	51.6	58.3	64.2	70.4	75.1	80.2
0.1	0.1	0.2	0.2	0.2	0.2	0.3	0.3	0.3	0.4	0.5	0.6	0.6	0.7
0.1	0.1	0.1	0.2	0.3	0.4	0.1	0.1	0.1	0.1	0.1	0.1	0.1	0.1
16.8	19.9	22.8	28.3	34.0	38.5	43.1	46.9	46.9	51.4	56.3	61.2	66.2	72.5
12.8	15.3	18.1	20.9	24.3	27.1	31.0	33.7	33.7	37.2	40.2	43.3	42.2	43.0
7.1	9.1	11.0	13.5	16.7	18.9	22.2	24.6	24.6	27.3	30.3	33.0	31.9	32.7
1.0	1.1	1.3	1.5	1.1	1.1	1.3	1.4	1.4	1.5	1.6	1.7	1.9	2.1
0.5	0.6	0.8	0.8	0.9	1.0	1.1	1.3	1.3	1.4	1.7	2.0	2.2	2.0
5.9	6.9	8.0	9.2	11.0	14.2	14.2	14.4	14.4	15.5	16.6	17.8	18.0	17.8
3.2	3.8	4.4	5.2	6.4	7.9	9.6	11.2	11.2	12.9	14.7	17.2	19.9	22.6
0.0	0.0	0.0	–	0.0	0.0	0.0	0.0	0.0	0.0	0.0	0.0	0.0	0.0
0.3	0.3	0.3	0.4	0.4	0.4	0.4	0.5	0.5	0.6	0.7	0.7	0.8	0.7
2.5	2.9	3.4	4.0	4.5	5.1	5.6	6.9	6.9	7.3	8.2	9.1	9.6	10.0
0.1	0.1	0.1	0,1	0.1	0.1	0.1	0.2	0.2	0.2	0.2	0.2	0.2	0.2
3.3	3.8	4.3	4.9	5.8	6.7	7.8	8.7	8.7	9.3	10.2	11.5	13.8	13.5
0.1	0.1	0.1	0.1	0.1	0.2	0.2	0.3	0.3	0.3	0.3	0.4	0.6	0.5
1.8	2.1	2.5	2.8	3.1	3.6	4.2	4.7	4.7	5.3	5.9	6.4	6.9	7.5 [a]
23.6	27.5	30.2	33.1	38.8	44.9	51.4	55.4	56.0	60.9	65.5	69.6	72.0	73.9
60.2	71.2	84.6	102.2	116.2	141.1	163.1	179.8	179.4	204.1	220.8	245.9	264.4	283.3
60.1	71.0	84.4	102.0	115.9	140.9	162.8	179.4	179.4	204.1	220.8	245.9	264.4	283.3
62.8	76.5	89.9	108.5	123.7	148.1	169.9	185.0	.	206.4	.	.	.	.

Table V–C
Capital transactions, transactions total and gross national product, 1965-1982
(billions of guilders)

	Source	1965	1966	1967	1968	1969
1. Real estate purchases	(CBS, Maandstat. Bouwnijverheid, Table 14.1)	2.0	2.0	2.3	3.1	3.0
2. Real stock exchange turnover	(CBS, Stat. Zakboek, Table O9)	3.6	2.9	6.5	14.3	14.7
3. Inheritances (net)	(CBS, Stat. Zakboek, Table S8)	1.7	1.8	1.8	1.9	2.1
4. Gifts	(CBS, Stat. Zakboek, Table S8)	0.4	0.2	0.2	0.2	0.2
5. Trade in second-hand cars	(RAI, Jaarverslag, Table 35)	1.6	1.9	2.0	2.5	2.4
6. Public issues	(CBS, Stat. Zakboek, Table O8)	2.2	2.2	2.2	2.4	2.8
7. Redemptions (excluding conversions)	(CBS, Stat. Zakboek, Table O8)	0.7	0.8	0.8	0.8	0.8
8. Repayments on mortgages	(DNB, Kwart.Ber.; CBS, Maandst. Fin.)	5.6	5.4	5.9	6.9	8.3
9. Repayments on consumer credit	(CBS, Stat. v.h. Cons. Krediet)	0.6	0.7	0.7	0.9	1.1
Total (1 inclusive to 9)		18.3	18.0	22.4	32.8	35.3
Sum total of all transactions		313.8	339.1	369.4	414.1	459.6
Ditto, adjusted for 1977 revision of National Accounts [b]		323.5	349.2	380.3	426.0	472.8
Cramer's estimate (1981a)		305.7	333.7	365.6	411.4	460.7
Gross national product		68.6	74.4	81.8	90.4	102.5
Ditto, adjusted for 1977 revision of National Accounts		72.1	78.3	86.1	95.1	107.8

[a] Provisional or estimated figure.

[b] Calculated as the sum total of the separate components adjusted where necessary for breaks in series.

1970	1971	1972	1973	1974	1975	1976	1977	1977	1978	1979	1980	1981	1982
3.7	5.1	6.5	7.7	8.2	11.7	15.1	20.1	20.1	24.0	18.9	16.9	14.2	12.0
15.5	16.1	28.5	25.7	16.4	24.6	28.9	36.5	36.5	42.7	38.7	49.8	55.1	92.5
2.2	2.4	2.4	2.8	3.0	3.6	3.6	4.0	4.0	5.4	5.8	5.3	4.3	4.3 [a]
0.2	0.2	0.2	0.4	0.5	0.4	0.4	0.5	0.5	0.9	1.0	1.1	1.4	1.4 [a]
3.0	3.1	3.4	3.7	3.9	5.2	5.8	6.4	6.4	7.0	7.2	7.2	6.8	7.8
3.0	3.7	3.4	2.3	3.3	6.0	5.0	7.0	7.0	7.1	7.7	11.5	15.0	22.9 [a]
0.9	1.0	1.0	0.9	1.1	1.5	2.2	2.6	2.6	2.8	3.9	4.7	6.0	7.7
9.4	10.7	11.5	16.7	18.3	18.9	35.9	37.8	37.8	49.1	37.0	29.2	47.7	34.6
1.2	1.5	1.7	2.0	2.2	2.7	4.2	4.2	4.2	4.8	4.7	4.5	4.4	4.2
39.1	43.8	58.7	62.1	56.8	74.6	101.0	119.2	119.2	143.8	125.0	130.2	154.9	187.4 [a]
518.9	579.6	649.9	741.5	841.0	941.1	1089.9	1189.3	1217.0	1328.9	1409.9	1530.3	1633.5	1713.1
533.4	595.5	667.7	762.0	863.0	964.6	1117.4	1217.0	1217.0	1328.9	1409.4	1530.3	1633.5	1713.1
519.4	588.0	666.1	760.0	862.3	970.1	1106.9	1221.6	.	1321.6	.	.	.	.
115.1	130.0	147.4	169.4	191.8	209.1	240.5	261.8	275.3	296.6	315.6	335.8	352.1	366.7
121.1	136.8	155.0	178.2	201.7	219.9	252.9	275.3	275.3	296.6	315.6	335.8	352.1	366.7

Appendix VI. Survey of estimates of the size of the black and the informal economies for a number of countries

Table VI-A comprises estimates of the size of the black economy for a number of countries as they can be found in the literature. For the sake of comparability, the survey is limited to 17 OECD countries. Incidentally, apart from figures for several East European countries, estimates exist only for Australia [9.6 % in 1978 according to Tucker (1980)], Israel and Colombia.

The estimates compiled from the literature have been subdivided in accordance with the estimation method used. The category 'other estimates' consists largely of educated guesses. Some authors have published several successive works in which sometimes strongly deviating estimations of the size of the black economy were found by means of the same method. In these cases the most recent estimate was chosen.

With regard to the survey, the following should be noted:

- Percentages which have been obtained via different methods are not directly comparable, because they relate to varying definitions of the black economy.
- For each estimation method, the percentages obtained for the different countries can also be compared only to a limited degree, because, for one thing, their national accounts take black activities into consideration in varying degrees.
- Except for the educated guesswork and Frey and Weck's (1983) rather dubious estimates, over 35 % of the 56 estimates have been obtained with the currency-ratio method or variants of that method. The most naïve of these, the Gutmann method, has been applied successfully only to the United States, Canada and Sweden. Attempts to apply this method to the Federal Republic of Germany, Denmark, France, Ireland, Norway and other countries, have led to implausible results.
- 27 % of the estimates were made with the aid of the fiscal or discrepancy method. In the case of the IRS study for the United States use was also made of results of tax auditing [5]. Contrary to results obtained with the above currency-ratio method, it turns out that the black economy measured with the fiscal method, expressed as a percentage of GNP, often decreases. The outcome is presumably distorted downwards as a result of the continuous improvements and adjustment in the national accounts.

---

[5] Other studies where this approximation method was used were those of the OECD (1981) and of the Swedish 'Riksskatterverk'. The 8-15 % tax evasion estimated in the latter for 1978 is, however, not translated into the size of the black economy expressed as a percentage of GNP, as is usual.

- Results derived from the outcome of surveys (13 %) usually prove to be the lowest. The question arises here to what extent this is caused by the fact that black income or expenditure is not disclosed, and non-response.
- The transactions method was applied to only four of the 17 countries. One of the main reasons for this lies in the data available. The estimates which, contrary to the currency-ratio method, take into consideration black transactions paid by means of transfers, are generally very high. With the exception of Feige's results for the United States, they show widely fluctuating developments.
- The estimates for Italy based on developments regarding the rate of participation in the labour market are the only estimates which also, in principle, comprise the barter economy.
- Frey and Weck's (1983) estimates made with the causal method, which can be found in the last column, are conditional upon the estimates obtained by Klovland (1980) via the currency-ratio method for Sweden and Norway. Klovland himself terms them unreliable. This is confirmed by the fact that the percentage found for Norway was adjusted downwards by 3 percentage points in a recent study made by Klovland in conjunction with other authors [Isachsen et al. (1982)]. This means that if the same applies to Sweden, all Frey and Weck's estimates would turn out to be 3 percentage points lower.

Table VI–A
Estimated size of the black or informal economy in 17 OECD countries
(% of GNP)

	Fiscal method			Survey - method [5]			Currency-ratio	
Austria								
Belgium	11.0	1970	Frank (1982)				15.2	1980
							20.8	1980
Canada							16.3	1976
							5.0-7.8	1976
							10.1	1980
Denmark	6.0	1974/75	Økonomiske Råd (1977)					
Federal Republic of Germany	8.9	1968	Albers (1974)				8.0	1978
	4.8	1974	Petersen (1982)				3.7	1980
Finland								
France	23.2	1965	Roze (1971)				6.7	1979
Ireland							8	1980
Italy							30	1978
Japan								
Netherlands	7	1977	CBS (1983b)					
Norway				2.3	1979	Isachsen et al. (1982)	9.2	1978
				3.0	1983	Isachsen et al. (1982)	6.3	1978
Spain							23	1978
Sweden	4.6	1978	Hansson (1980)	0.5	1979	SIFO (1981)	9.3-12.4	1976
	3-7	1970/80	Hansson (1982)				13.2	1978
Switzerland	15.1	1978	Ernst (1983)				3.7	1980
United Kingdom	3.3	1978	Macafee (1980)	2.3-3	1977	Dilnot/Morris (1981)	3.3-11.0	1979
	2	1970/80	O'Higgins (1982)	2.5-2.9	1977	O'Higgins (1980)		
				4	1977	O'Higgins (1982)		
United States	5.8-7.9	1976	IRS (1979) [1]	1.4	1981	Smith (1983b)	10.2	1976
	3.9	1977	Park (1979)				2.9-4.9	1978
	5	1978	Lehman (1979)				14-28	1979
	3.5-4.0	1982	Parker (1982)					

Explanatory note
The name of an author followed by a year refers to a publication included in the bibliography.

1 Partly based on the results of tax auditing.

2 Unless stated otherwise, the estimates shown in this column were obtained with the Tanzi method where the currency ratio – or the currency itself – is made dependent on a number of variables. The estimates presented are all conditional upon the burden of taxation in the base year chosen by the author.

3 Based on a constant ratio of cash to demand deposits (Gutmann method).

4 Based on a change in income and price elasticities in a demand for currency function estimated for two separate periods.

methods [2]	Transactions method			Other estimates and educated guesses			Frey 1978 [8]
				3.8	1976	Franz (1983) [6]	8.9
Mont (1982)							12.1
Geeroms (1983)							
Mirus/Smith (1981) [3]							
Mirus/Smith (1981)	23.6	1978	Mirus/Smith (1981)				8.7
Mirus/Smith (1982) [4]	14.5	1980	Mirus/Smith (1982)				
							11.8
Kirchgässner (1981)	27	1980	Langfeldt (1982)				8.6
Langfeldt (1982)							
							7.6
Barthélemy (1982)							9.4
Boyle (1982)							7.2
Saba (1980)				14-20	1977	Contini (1981) [5]	11.4
				25-33	1977	Martino (1980) [5]	
				20	1978	Forte (1979)	
				14	1979	Alvaro (1979)	
							4.1
				4	1978	Langman (1978)	9.6
				5	1979	Broesterhuizen (1983) [11]	
				4.2	1981	Sleurink (1982)	
Klovland (1980)				4-6	1983	Isachsen et al. (1983)	9.2
Isachsen a.o. (1982)							
Lafuente (1980)							6.5
Veckans Affärer (1978) [3]							13.2
Klovland (1980)							
Frey/Weck (1983)				2.7	1975	Frey/Weck (1983) [11]	4.3
Matthews (1981)	15	1979	Feige (1981)	7.5	1979	Pile (1979)	8.0
				4.0-7.2		Rose (1983) [11]	
Gutmann (1977) [3]	27	1979	Feige (1980)	6.4-11.5	1980	Simon/Witte (1982) [7]	
Tanzi (1982)				4-6	1982	Tanzi (1982)	8.3
Feige (1980) [3]				2.8	1976	Blades (1982) [9]	
				1.5	1976	OECD (1981) [10]	

5 Based on the rate of participation in the labour market.

6 Obtained by comparing and combining various statistics (mostly regarding to labour market).

7 Based on sector analysis, tax auditing.

8 Results for 1978 of Frey and Weck's (1983) causal method, based on outcomes found by Klovland (1980) for Sweden and Norway.

9 Obtained by combining estimations made by others: concealed legal production (2.2 %) + illegal production (1.5 %) + theft by employees (0.5 %) – concealed production included in GNP (1.5 %).

10 Based on tax auditing.

11 Based on analysis of fraud-sensitivity.

Bibliography

Albers, W., 1974, Umverteilungswirkungen der Einkommenssteuer, in: W. Albers (ed.), *Öffentliche Finanzwirtschaft und Verteilung* II, Berlin, Duncker & Humblot, pp. 69-144.

Alvaro, G., 1979, L'Italia sommersa che non paga le tasse, *Mondoperaio* 32, February, pp. 62-65.

Barthélemy, P., 1982, *The underground economy in France*, paper presented at the International Conference on the Unobserved Sector, NIAS, Wassenaar, June 3-6.

Battelle - Institut e.v., 1976, *World-wide investigation of attitudes towards payment methods and forecast of the demand for new payment systems*, Battelle-Institut e.v., Frankfurt.

Bijsterveld, W.J. van, 1980, *Aangepaste versie van het verslag van een onderzoek naar de aard en de omvang van de belastingfraude*, ISMO, 's-Gravenhage, april.

Blades, D.W., 1982, The hidden economy and national accounts, *OECD Observer*, January, pp. 15-17.

Blades, D.W., 1983, *Crime: what should be included in the national accounts and what difference it would make* , paper presented at the Conference on The Economics of the Shadow Economy, Bielefeld, October 10-14.

Blokland, J., 1982, Het officieuze circuit: een nadere begripsbepaling, CBS, *Statistisch Magazine* 2, no. 2, pp. 4-9.

Boyle, G.E., 1982, *A glimpse at the non-accounted economy: the case of Ireland*, paper presented at the International Conference on the Unobserved Economy, NIAS, Wassenaar, June 3-6.

Broesterhuizen, G.A.A.M., 1983, *The unobserved sector and the national accounts in the Netherlands*, CBS, note 395-83-PS.E8, August.

Butter, F.A.G. den, Coenen R.L., 1981, Het bankbiljet als produkt, *Economisch Statistische Berichten* 66, pp. 162-167.

Cagan, P., 1958, The demand for currency relative to total money supply, *The Journal of Political Economy* 66, pp. 303-328.

CBS, 1983a, *Zwarte aktiviteiten en de nationale rekeningen*, CBS, note 416-83-H.E8, September.

CBS, 1983b, *Vergelijking van gegevens over het inkomen van gezinshuishoudingen uit fiscale bron en uit de nationale rekeningen; resultaten over 1977 met bijzondere aandacht voor ontvangen rente*, CBS, Voorburg/Heerlen, November.

Clotfelter, C.T., 1983, Tax evasion and tax rates: an analysis of individual returns, *The Review of Economics and Statistics* 65, no. 3, pp. 363-373.

Contini, B., 1979, *Lo sviluppo di un'economia parallela*, Edizione di Comunità, Milano.

Contini, B., 1981, The second economy of Italy, *Journal of Contemporary Studies* 4, no. 3; reprinted in: Tanzi, V. (ed.), 1982, *The underground economy in the United States and abroad*, Lexington Books, pp. 199-208.

Cramer, J.S., 1978, De omvang van het betalingsverkeer en de omloopsnelheid van het geld: enige ramingen voor 1974-1977, in: Klant, J.J., Driehuis, W. en Bierens, H.J. (ed.), *Samenleving en onderzoek*, Stenfert Kroese, Leiden, pp. 209-223.

Cramer, J.S., 1980, *The regular and irregular circulation of money in the United States*, Faculty of Actuarial Science & Econometrics, University of Amsterdam, A&E Report 11/80.

Cramer, J.S., 1981a, The work money does; the transaction velocity of circulation of money in the Netherlands, 1950-1978, *European Economic Review* 15, pp. 307-326.

Cramer, J.S., 1981b, Co-referaat bij inleiding van prof.dr. E. Feige: Theory and measurement of the unobserved economy, *Openbare Uitgaven* 13, no. 4, pp. 173-175.

Cramer, J.S., 1982, Contanten - wit, zwart, onzichtbaar, *Kwantitatieve Methoden* no. 9, 1982, pp. 2-28.

Dilnot, A. Morris, C.N., 1981, What do we know about the black economy?, *Fiscal Studies* 2, no. 1, pp. 58-73, reprinted in Tanzi, V. (ed.), 1982, *The underground economy in the United States and abroad*, Lexington Books, pp. 163-179.

Van Eck, R., 1983, Secundaire aktiviteiten en de nationale rekeningen, *CBS Select* 2, CBS, 's-Gravenhage, Staatsuitgeverij, pp. 195-216.

Ernst, V., 1983, *Die Wohlstandverteilung in der Schweiz*, Rüegger, Diessenhofen.

Fase, M.M.G., Van Nieuwkerk, M., 1976, The banknote circulation in the Netherlands since 1900; prospect and retrospect, De Nederlandsche Bank N.V., *Quarterly Statistics* 1976 no. 1, pp. 12-22.

Fase, M.M.G., Van Nieuwkerk, M., 1977, The demand for banknotes in four countries; a statistical analysis for the Netherlands, the Federal Republic of Germany, Switzerland and the United States of America, De Nederlandsche Bank N.V., *Quarterly Statistics* 1977 no. 1, pp. 84-98.

Fase, M.M.G., 1979, *Liquiditeitsquote en zwart circuit*, mimeo DNB, 25 January 1979.

Feige, E.L., 1979, How big is the irregular economy?, *Challenge*, November-December.

Feige, E.L., 1980, *A new perspective on macroeconomic phenomena, the theory and measurement of the unobserved sector of the United States economy: causes, consequences and implications*, paper, Madison/Leiden.

Feige, E.L., 1981, The UK's unobserved economy: a preliminary asessment, *Journal of Economic Affairs* 2, no. 3, pp. 164-171.

Fisher, I., 1909, A new method of estimating the velocity of circulation of money, *Journal of the Royal Statistical Society* 72, pp. 604-618.

Fisher, N.W.E., 1982, *An expenditure approach to the estimation of the hidden economy and informal labour market*, working paper 11, Bureau of Labour Market Research, Canberra City.

Forte, F., 1979, Lo scandalo fiscale: i conti dell economia sommersa, *Mondoperaio* 32, febbraio, pp. 67-68.

Frank, M., 1976, Fraude des revenus soumis a l'impôt des personnes physiques et perte d'impôt qui en résulte pour le Trésor-Etude méthodologique, *Public Finance* 31, no. 1, pp. 1-30.

Frank, M., 1977, *La fraude fiscale en Belgique*, Editions de l'Université Libre, Bruxelles.

Frank, M., 1982, *Essay on the unrecorded economy by the fiscal approach and its incidence on income and wealth distribution in Belgium*, paper presented at the Eighteenth General Conference of the IARIW, Luxembourg, August 21-27.

Franz, A., 1983, *Estimates of the hidden economy in Austria on the basis of official statistics*, paper presented at the Eighteenth General Conference of the IARIW, Luxembourg, August 21-27.

Frey, B.S., Weck, H., 1981, What produces a hidden economy?, An international cross section analysis, *Southern Economic Journal* 49, no. 3, pp. 822-832.

Frey, B.S., Weck, H., Pommerehne, W.W., 1982, Has the shadow economy grown in Germany? an exploratory study, *Weltwirtschaftliches Archiv* 118, Heft 3, pp. 499-524.

Frey, B.S., 1982, *The shadow economy in the politico-economic system: implications for measurement and policy*, paper presented at the International Conference on the Unobserved Sector, NIAS, Wassenaar, June 3 - 6.

Frey, B.S., Weck, H., 1983, *Measuring the shadow economy: the case of Switzerland*, paper presented at the Conference on The Economics of the Shadow Economy, Bielefeld, October 10-14.

Geeroms, H., 1983, De ondergrondse economie in België, *Tijdschrift voor Economie en Management* 28, no. 1, pp. 77-91.

Gutmann, P.M., 1977, The subterranean economy, *Financial Analysts Journal*, November/ December, pp. 26-28.

Hansson, I., 1980, Sverige's svarta sektor, *Ekonomisk Debatt* 8, pp. 595-602.

Hansson, I., 1982, The underground economy in a high tax country: the case of Sweden, in: Tanzi, V. (ed.), 1982, *The underground economy in the United States and abroad*, Lexington Books, pp. 233-243.

Heertje, A., Cohen, H., 1980, *Het officieuze circuit: een witboek over zwart en grijs geld*, Het Spectrum, Utrecht.

Holtrop, M.W., 1928, *De omloopsnelheid van het geld*, Paris, Amsterdam.

IRS (Internal Revenue Service), 1979, *Estimates of income unreported on individual income tax returns*, publication 1104, Washington, D.C., Government Printing Office, September.

Isachsen, A.J., Klovland, J.T., Strøm, S., 1982, The hidden economy in Norway, in: Tanzi, V. (ed.), 1982, *The underground economy in the United States and abroad*, Lexington Books, pp. 209-231.

Isachsen, A.J., Strøm, S., 1983, *The size and growth of the hidden economy in Norway*, paper presented at the Eighteenth General Conference of the IARIW, Luxembourg, August 21-27.

Jonker, R., 1973, Raming van de transacties in Nederland, *Economisch Statistische Berichten* (July 25), pp. 675-676.

Kirchgässner, G., 1981, *Verfahren zur Erfassung der Grösse und Entwicklung des Schattensektors*, Eidgenössische Technische Hochschule Zürich, November.

Klovland, J.T., 1980, *In search of the hidden economy: tax evasion and the demand for currency in Norway and Sweden*, discussion paper 18/80, Norwegian School for Economics and Business Administration, Bergen.

Lafuente, A., 1980, Una medición de la economia oculta en Espana, *Boletin de Estudios Económicos*, pp. 581-593.

Langfeldt, E., 1982, *The unobserved economy in the Federal Republic of Germany: a preliminary assessment*, paper presented at the International Conference on the Unobserved Sector, NIAS, Wassenaar, June 3-6.

Langman, H., 1978, Opmerkingen over zwart circuit en werkgelegenheid in *Rede voor de Maatschappij voor Nijverheid en Handel in Rotterdam op 24 oktober 1978.*

Laurent, R.D., 1970, *Currency transfer by denomination*, Ph. D. thesis, University of Chicago.

Lehman, S.C., 1979, Relationship between personal income and taxable income, 1947-74, *Survey of Current Business*, December, p. 17.

Macafee, K., 1980, A glimpse of the hidden economy in the national accounts, *Economic Trends*, No. 316, Central Statistical Office, February, pp. 81-87; reprinted in Tanzi, V. (ed.), 1982, *The underground economy in the United States and abroad*, Lexington Books, pp. 147-161.

Martino, A., 1980, *Another Italian economic miracle*, paper, Mont Pelerin Society, Stanford Conference.

Matthews, K., 1981, The demand for currency and the rise of black economy 1973-1979, Liverpool, *Research Group Economic Bulletin* 2.

Mirus, R., Smith, R.S., 1981, Canada's irregular economy, *Canadian Public Policy - Analyse de Politiques* 7-3, pp. 444-453; reprinted in: Tanzi, V. (ed.), 1982, *The underground economy in the United States and abroad*, Lexington Books, pp. 273-284.

Mirus, R., Smith, R.S., 1982, *The unobserved economy: Canada*, paper presented at the International Conference on the Unobserved Sector, NIAS, Wassenaar, June 3-6.

Molevski, B., 1982, America's Underground Economy, in: Tanzi, V. (ed.), 1982, The underground economy in the United States and abroad, Lexington Books, pp. 47-67.

Mont, J., 1982, De zwarte aktiviteiten in België: oorzaken, omvang en implicaties, *Tijdschrift voor Economie en Management* 27, no. 3, pp. 259-273.

Niesten, L.J., 1968, Het betalingsverkeer en de Postcheque- en Girodienst, *Een halve eeuw Post Cheque en Girodienst*, Het Spectrum, Utrecht, pp.89-103.

OECD, 1981, *The hidden economy in the context of the national accounts*, mimeo, DES/NI/ 81.3, Paris, April.

O'Higgins, M., 1980, *Measuring the hidden economy: a review of evidence and methodologies*, paper, Outer Circle Policy Unit, London, July.

O'Higgins, M., 1982, *Assessing the underground economy in the United Kingdom*, paper presented at the International Conference on the Unobserved Economy, NIAS, Wassenaar, June 3-6.

O'Higgins, M., 1983, *The relationship between the formal and hidden economies: an explanatory analysis for four countries*, paper presented at the Conference on The Economics of the Shadow Economy, Bielefeld, October 10-14.

Økonomiske Råd, 1977, *Dansk økonomi*, Statens Tryknings Kontor, Kopenhagen.

Park, T., 1979, *Reconciliation between personal income and taxable income, 1947-1977*, paper prepared for the Bureau of Economic Analysis, Washington D.C., May.

Parker, R., 1982, Presentation to the Federal Statistics Users Conference, November; cited in: Feige, E.L., Mc.Gee, R.T., *Employment trends and supply side estimates of the unobserved sector of the U.S. economy*, paper presented at the Eighteenth General Conference of the IARIW, Luxembourg, August 21-27.

Pen, J., 1983, Morfologie van het zwarte gebeuren, *De Gids,* 146, no. 2/3 , pp. 115-125.

Petersen, H.G., 1982, Size of the public sector, economic growth and the informal economy: development trends in the Federal Republic of Germany, *The Review of Income and Wealth* 28, no. 2, pp. 191-215.

Pile, Sir W., (House of Commons), 1979, *Evidence of Sir William Pile* (former Chairman of the United Kingdom's Board of Inland Revenue), Public Expenditure Committee, March 26.

Rose, R., 1983, Getting by three economies: the resources of the official, unofficial and domestic economies, *Studies in Public Policy* 110, University of Strthclyde.

Roze, H., 1971, Prestations sociales, impôt direct et cellule de revenus, *Economie et Statistique* 20 (February), pp. 3-14.

Saba, A., 1980, *L'Industria Sommersa,* Padua, Marsilio, 1980.

SIFO, 1981, *Svartbetalare och svartjabbare,* mimeo, SIFO, Stockholm, January.

Simon, C.P., Witte, A.D., (with Eakin, K., Schoettler, R.C., Ziegert, A.L.), 1982, *Beating the system: the underground economy,* Auburn House Publishing Company, Boston/ Massachusetts.

Sleurink, H., 1982, *Hoe fraude de samenleving bedreigt; het ISMO-rapport,* Gouda Quint, Arnhem.

Smith, J.D., 1983a, *Omitted product in the U.S. National Accounts: the grey economy,* paper presented at Eighteenth General Conference of the IARIW, Luxembourg, August 21-27.

Smith, J.D., 1983b, *Market motives in the informal economy,* paper presented at the Conference on The Economics of the Shadow Economy, Bielefeld, October 10-14.

Tanzi, V., 1980, The underground economy in the United States: estimates and implications, *Banca Nazionale de Lavoro Quarterly Review* 135 (December), pp. 427-453; reprinted (with proscript) in Tanzi, V. (ed.), 1982, *The underground economy in the United States and abroad,* Lexington/Massachusetts/Toronto, Lexington Books, pp. 69-92.

Tanzi, V., 1982, A second (and more skeptical) look at the underground economy of the United States, in: Tanzi, V., (ed.); *The underground economy in the United States and abroad,* Lexington Books, pp. 103-118.

Tucker, M., 1980, The underground economy in Australia, *Economic Review,* The Commercial Bank of Australia Limited, September; reprinted in: Tanzi, V., (ed.), *The underground economy in the United States and abroad,* Lexington Books, pp. 215-322.

Van Tuinen, H.K., 1980, *Verwarring over officieuze geldcircuits nog groter,* NRC/Handelsblad, December 1.

Van Tuinen, H.K., 1981, Co-referaat bij inleiding van prof.dr. E. Feige tijdens de bijeenkomst van de Vereniging voor Openbare Financiën op 5 juni 1981 te Den Haag, *Openbare Uitgaven* 13, no. 4, pp. 168-185.

Uyttewaal, R.A.I.M., 1981, *Maandelijkse indexcijfers van de betalingen met Nederlandse bankbiljetten van 1966 tot 1980,* Instituut voor Actuariaat en Econometrie, Universiteit van Amsterdam, A & E note 1981/1.

Veckans Affärer, 1978, Nytt sätt at mäta dolda economin: nära 10 procen av BNP är svart, *Veckans Affärer* 22 (June 1), pp. 11-13.

Zijlstra, J., 1948, *De omloopsnelheid van het geld en zijn betekenis voor geldwaarde en monetair evenwicht*, Stenfert Kroese, Leiden.

Authors Index

Albers, W., 66
Alvaro, G., 67
Barthélemy, P., 67
Batelle-Institut e.v., 25
Bijsterveld, W.J. van, 10
Blades, D.W., 13, 67
Blokland, J., 9n, 12n
Boyle, G.E., 67
Broesterhuizen, G.A.A.M., 12, 13n, 67
Butter, F.A.G. den, Coenen, R.L., 42n
Cagan, P., 14
CBS, 9, 10, 11, 66
Clotfelder, C.T., 12
Contini, B., 67
Cramer, J.S., 9n, 10, 18n, 19, 20, 21, 23n, 25, 52, 53, 54, 55, 56
Dilnot, A., Morris, C.N., 66
Eck, R. van, 9n
Ernst, V., 66
Fase, M.M.G., 26n
Fase, M.M.G., Van Nieuwkerk, M., 45
Feige, E.L., 9, 12n, 15, 30n, 36, 65, 67
Fisher, I., 15, 19, 21
Fisher, N.W.E., 13n
Forte, F., 67
Frank, M., 11, 66
Franz, A., 67
Frey, B.S., 13
Frey, B.S., Weck, H., 13, 18n, 35, 58, 64, 65, 67
Geeroms, H., 67
Gutmann, P.M., 14, 15, 67
Hansson, I., 66
Heertje, A., Cohen, H., 9n, 10
Holtrop, M.W., 16n
IRS, 11, 14, 66
Isachsen, A.J. et al., 12, 65, 66, 67
Jonker, R., 55
Kirchgässner, G., 67
Klovland, J.T., 65, 67
Lafuente, A., 67
Langfeldt, E., 67
Langman, H., 67
Laurent, R.D., 19, 21, 42
Lehman, S.C., 66
Macafee, K., 66
Martino, A., 67
Matthews, K., 67
Mirus, R., Smith, R.S., 15, 67
Molevsky, B., 27n
Mont, J., 67
Niesten, L.J., 55
OECD, 65n, 67
O'Higgins, M., 27n, 66
Økonomiske Råd, 66
Park, T., 66
Parker, R., 66
Pen, J., 9n
Petersen, H.G., 66
Pile, W., 67
Riksskatteverk, 65n
Rose, R., 13n, 67
Roze, H., 66
Saba, A., 67
SIFO, 66
Simon, C.P., Witte, A.D., 67
Sleurink, H., 67
Smith, J.D., 66
Tanzi, V., 9n, 12
Tucker, M., 64
Tuinen, H.K. van, 9n, 12
Uyttewaal, R.A.I.M., 19, 4c
Zijlstra, J., 16n, 18n

Subject Index

Amplification of bank transfers, 24, 25, 30, 50
Barter transactions, 9, 13n, 65
Black economy, 9ff
Burden of taxation and social security contributions, 10, 13
Capital transactions, 18, 29, 56-59, 62, 63
Cash loop, 19-21, 23, 30
Cash loop method, 19, 20, 23
Cash payments, 19-23, 36, 43, 44
Cash withdrawals, 19, 20, 53n
Causal method, 13, 35, 64
Circulation formula, 43
Circulation of coins, 21
Criminal activities, 13
Currency-ratio method, 14, 35, 64
Current transactions, 31, 32, 55, 56
Determinants of black economy, 13
Direct methods, 11-13
Discrepancy method, 11, 64
Estimates for other countries, 34, 35, 64, 67
Estimation methods, 11-15
Financial innovation, 23, 40
Financial transactions, 18, 25
Fiscal method, 11, 64
Fraud-sensitive, 12, 28
GNP, 27, 62, 63
Gutmann-method, 14, 15
Income transfers, 18, 28, 56, 60, 61
Identity of exchange, 15
Indirect methods, 11, 13-15
Informal economy, 9ff
Integration of production process, 16
Intrabank transfers, 23, 47
Italian method, 13n, 16
Intensity of use of banknotes, 21, 45
Lifetime, 21, 30, 44, 45
Lifetime method, 19, 21, 23
Modified transactions method, 31, 32
Monetary methods, 11, 13-15
Non-current transactions, 17, 18, 28, 29
Outgoing transfers, 23, 47
Output public sector, 28, 55-59
Payments to foreign countries, 24, 25, 27
Payments per banknote, G, 21, 43, 44
Sensitivity analysis, 12, 13
Surveys, 12, 65
Tanzi-method, 14, 15, 35
Tax-auditing, 26
Transactions method, 9, 15-18
Transactions total PT, 15ff
Transactions velocity, 21, 39
Transfers, 23
Transfers at Bank's Clearing Institution, 23
Transfers at the Netherlands Bank, 23, 24
Transfers central government, 24, 25
Transfers system, 23, 47, 48
Transfers to other deposits, 28, 29
Turnover rate, 20
Volume of payments MV, 15ff

GPSR Compliance

The European Union's (EU) General Product Safety Regulation (GPSR) is a set of rules that requires consumer products to be safe and our obligations to ensure this.

If you have any concerns about our products, you can contact us on ProductSafety@springernature.com

In case Publisher is established outside the EU, the EU authorized representative is:

Springer Nature Customer Service Center GmbH
Europaplatz 3
69115 Heidelberg, Germany

Batch number: 10830943

Printed by Printforce, the Netherlands